NIGHT OF THE LONG KNIVES

HITLER'S EXCISION OF RÖHM'S SA BROWNSHIRTS
30 JUNE – 2 JULY 1934

PHIL CARRADICE

Pen & Sword
MILITARY

Schutzstaffel (SS) knives: 'Loyalty is My Honour'. (Photo Biso)

First published in Great Britain in 2018 by
PEN AND SWORD MILITARY
an imprint of
Pen and Sword Books Ltd
47 Church Street
Barnsley
South Yorkshire S70 2AS

Copyright © Phil Carradice, 2018

ISBN 978 1 526728 93 7

Typeset by Aura Technology and Software Services, India
Printed and bound in Malta by Gutenberg

Pen & Sword Books Ltd incorporates the imprints of Pen & Sword
Archaeology, Atlas, Aviation, Battleground, Discovery, Family History, History, Maritime, Military, Naval,
Politics, Railways, Select, Social History, Transport, True Crime, Claymore Press, Frontline Books, Leo
Cooper, Praetorian Press, Remember When, Seaforth Publishing and Wharncliffe.

For a complete list of Pen and Sword titles please contact
Pen and Sword Books Limited
47 Church Street, Barnsley, South Yorkshire, S70 2AS, England
email: enquiries@pen-and-sword.co.uk
website: www.pen-and-sword.co.uk

CONTENTS

Dachau concentration camp, the final resting place for many SA victims, seen here after liberation in 1945. (U.S. Holocaust Museum)

INTRODUCTION

"I ask you now, is any little thing like being damned eternally a satisfactory excuse for behaving like a complete rat?"

Fritz Leiber

It is a sad but unmistakeable fact that Adolf Hitler, over seven decades since his diabolical regime came crashing down in flames, still retains the power to fascinate. Quite why this should be remains something of an enigma. Perhaps it is the depth of the man's evil, a stunning and bottomless cavern that glares up at you whenever you gaze in; perhaps it is the way millions bowed to his every word, worshipping and obeying without thought or regret; perhaps it is just that all evil resonates and when we look at it, safe from the comfort and security of our armchairs, we can heave a sigh of relief and then pass on to other things.

Bad has always been good or a good seller at least. It's the reason we remember Fagin, Bill Sykes and the Artful Dodger but can barely relate to wimpy Oliver Twist. It's why we delight in the activities of Jaws, Darth Vader, Count Dracula, Hannibal Lecter and so many more—not because they are particularly attractive but because they are so consummately bad. We might hope for some degree of redemption for them and that does, sometimes, occur. As they used to say in the old *Wells Fargo* TV series of the 1950s: "There's a little good in the worst of us, a little bad in the best." But really the vileness and villainies of those archetypal baddies are so all-consuming that they make us feel rather good—and safe.

Adolf Hitler fits that bill perfectly. And yet there remains an air of mystery about him and his followers. Can anybody really be that evil? Could things have been different

Adolf Hitler, already hell bent on destruction.

if he had chosen a different route, a different path? There is no answer but it is all part of the fascination.

The Night of the Long Knives was a seminal moment for Hitler and the Nazis. Before that deadly weekend when Hitler destroyed the last vestiges of opposition to his regime, the Nazi Party had been comprised of thugs, vicious and violent thugs admittedly, but thugs all the same. They were men who lived by the fist and the jackboot without fear of reprisal. After the purge they were cold-blooded murderers who would stop at nothing to achieve their ends. As the 1930s progressed it was almost as if the demands of an obscene regime superseded the equally vile intentions of individuals. At its most basic level the aims and ideals of individuals were subsumed by the needs of the State.

Individuals still committed atrocities but they were approved, even directed, by the government—in fact by Adolf Hitler. And all of the horrors of the Third Reich, the persecutions and the Holocaust, the terrible wars and the destruction, stem from Hitler and from that moment in the warm and unsuspecting early summer of 1934.

The underlying causes or motives behind the killing of several hundred potential opponents to Hitler were not just the needs of Germany or the Party; there was also a personal element for Germany's new dictator. The Night of the Long Knives was a watershed, a crucial moment when he stood poised between the pull of friendship and the desire for power, ultimate and absolute power which, as we know, corrupts absolutely. We also know which way Hitler chose to go.

There is only one purpose or aim behind studying history: to make sure that we do not make the same mistakes again. Sadly, we do not have to look far in this world to find governments and individuals who have not learned from their reading of history and continue to make the same old errors over and over again. We all of us have a duty, as strange and as abstract as it might seem, to ensure that people study history for the right reasons. If we can make that study interesting in the way that a story is interesting, holding us rapt and fascinated from beginning to end, then we have a much better chance of fulfilling that aim.

We should all read about this dire and dreadful weekend of murder and mayhem, viewing it as a terrible story at the start of an even more terrible period in human history. Asking any reader to enjoy the tale of murder and betrayal, the double dealing that makes up a large and significant part of the Night of the Long Knives, would be both facile and wrong. It would make us little better than the Nazis who committed the outrages in the first place. But that should not stop people learning from those dreadful events. It is, perhaps, not what Adolf Hitler would have wanted but, then, as Hitler and the Nazis eventually found out, we do not always get what we want in life.

Hitler and Ernst Röhm, friends but also mortal enemies.

OVERTURE

In the game of golf there is an expression used to describe that infuriating moment when a ball hit across the green comes to rest, hovering on the lip of the hole. It is called 'a banana republic'. In other words just one more revolution is all that is needed for the ball to topple forward and finish up at the bottom of the cup.

In the early months of 1934 Hitler's Germany was very far from being a 'banana republic' but his revolution was not yet secure. Elements within the Party, notably the leadership of the Sturmabteilung (the SA as it was known), felt that things had not gone far enough. The revolution had taken place but it had stopped short of achieving all that many Party members wanted and, more importantly, expected.

These men, most of them on the left wing of the Party, believed that while the nationalist aspect of the Nazi manifesto had undoubtedly been implemented, the socialist ideals of the movement—socialist ideals that had attracted the working classes in their thousands during the 1920s—had not been given proper attention. In fact they had been ignored. Hitler himself had designed and drawn up the Nazi manifesto in the early 1920s. That did not mean an awful lot to Party members, leaders

The straight-arm Nazi salute, perhaps the most symbolic and terrifying gesture of the 1930s and 1940s.

and rank and file alike. The manifesto was basic and had little relevance either to the aims of the Nazis or to the political and economic situation in Germany. It was simply a sop, something that Hitler contrived in order to woo the working-class masses. He had no more belief or interest in socialism than he did in democracy and the same could be said for most of the other members of his Party.

In effect, apart from men like Ernst Röhm, the two Strasser brothers and one or two other similar thinkers, nobody paid the slightest attention to the manifesto, consigning the document to the top shelf of the bookcase or even the waste basket. Throughout the years of the Third Reich that manifesto did not change, not from the moment of its creation until the destruction of the Party in 1945; not because it was so significant or important but, rather, because it meant so little. The manifesto, like so much else about the Nazi Party, was a total sham.

Nevertheless, in the early days of the movement there were Nazis who believed in it implicitly, men who were convinced that National Socialism was an ideology, not just a means to an end for people like Adolf Hitler. That was why they had joined the Party, after all. Senior Party members such as Ernst Röhm, commander of the SA, and Gregor Strasser, possibly the most able and intelligent of all the National Socialists, were classic examples.

The Nazi Party has often been accused of being essentially a middle-class movement. It was the party of the small tenant farmer, the teacher, the minor businessman or the office clerk whose savings had been suddenly wiped out by the economic crash of the 1920s. To some extent that was true but it was also the groundswell of support from working men and women—or perhaps, during the Depression years, that should be the *not* working men and women—that had given Hitler's dream the impetus to succeed.

The middle classes may have paid their Party subscriptions and may have attended rallies and listened intently to speeches from the Leader—der Führer as they called him from a very early stage, even though he was not technically deserving of the title until he achieved ultimate power in 1933.

By and large, however, the middle classes did not make up the rank and file of the SA and they were certainly not the types to battle with sticks and bottles, guns and knives, against hardened Communist agitators. Armchair fascists would probably be too strong a description but they were certainly not the street battlers that Hitler needed.

Come to that, neither was every working class member of the Nazi Party. Most of these were respectable individuals with or without jobs, with or without family, but all of them interested in the regeneration of the country. As such they were not very different from many other motivated members of political parties the world over. For the urban warfare that was endemic across Germany in the 1920s you needed

The SA was comprised of street fighters and thugs. This contemporary magazine cover shows that injuries to those involved in the fighting was a two-way processes.

very special skills, very special types of people.

In particular you needed hard men, physically tough men who had spent years at the coal face or enduring the heat of the Ruhr blast furnaces. You needed men who had risked death daily on docks like Hamburg and Rotterdam or who had bent their heads against the winter wind and snow as they manhandled barges up and down the Rhine. But even that was not really enough.

To provide that little extra thrust and to win the battle of the streets you needed enforcers, out-of-work bouncers and bully boys whose initial response to any problem was to lash out with their fists and feet or with any weapon that came easily to hand. You needed thugs who were physically and emotionally as tough as teak, hard and violent men like Emil Maurice, Ulrich Graf and especially Ernst Röhm. All three of them were early members of the Nazi Party and of the SA. They are men you will meet in the pages of this book.

In those post-war days the working classes across the world were beginning to flex their muscles. They had fought the 'war to end all wars' and had died in their millions, not to keep their lords and masters in wealth and power but to gain at least some measure of control over their own destinies. The economic depression had, unfortunately, destroyed that dream and with little else to cheer them, many of these disappointed workers turned to extremist groups like the Nazi Party in the hope that extremist views might just lead to extremist solutions.

The Nazis had changed their name from the German Workers' Party to The National Socialist German Workers' Party (Nazi for short) in February 1920, deliberately trying to appeal to all elements of German society. Hitler knew, even in these early days when the emphasis was more on the bullet than the ballot, that the blue-collar vote or presence was essential to success. He needed to bring working men into the Party.

Bringing them in was one thing; keeping them was another. Socialism might be emblazoned there in the name of the organization, Ernst Röhm and other SA leaders now pointed out, but it was mere tokenism, a pointless exercise, if the upper echelons of the Party refused to do anything about it when given the chance.

Röhm, chief of staff for the SA, was a strange, contradictory man. Violent, dictatorial, challenging, he was also openly homosexual at a time when popular opinion—and Hitler's opinion in particular—was opposed to love between men and women of the same gender. Röhm could be charming but like Hitler his temper was quick, anger and aggression lying only skin deep and always liable to erupt with very little reason or cause.

Whatever his sexual propensities and despite his vicious anti-Semitism, Röhm did hold genuine socialist values—twisted and unique to him, perhaps, but socialist nonetheless—which might, at first, seem at odds with the aims and attitudes of many Nazis. With Röhm there was no denying that they were genuine enough.

The problem facing Hitler in the early 1930s was not just ideological either. Apart from the 'thinkers' of the Left, the Party was full of less esoteric men and these also needed catering to. There were large numbers, particularly in the brawling, rabble-rousing SA, who had been expecting financial and economic reward once Hitler came to power. It had always been implicit in the Nazi message—you have been unfairly treated but, come the revolution, there will be a realignment of riches and power. Stick with us,

Ernst Röhm salutes, Hitler preens.

kid, was the message Hitler and his myrmidons seemed to be propounding, stick with us and you'll be all right.

It was a long time coming, the success that Hitler had promised; three steps forward and two back every time. But they stuck with him, revelling in the idea that if they could not improve their standard of living or quality of life, they could at least look forward to breaking a few skulls every time they put on the brown shirts that soon became their trademark uniform.

Despite the heady euphoria of January and February 1933 when power was at last handed to the Nazi Party, little changed for such men. Despite the promises and expectations, after that high-water mark the doling out of sinecures and patronage had been limited in the extreme.

Put quite simply, those Brownshirts or Stormtroopers who had battled the police, the Communists, the Socialists and other fringe groups, men who had suffered on the streets of the country's cities during the hungry twenties, wanted more—they wanted back pay for their efforts. And so far they had not had it.

When they looked at the leadership they saw Hitler, Hess, Göring and the rest hobnobbing with the men of the establishment, taking afternoon tea and enjoying fine wines—not that Hitler ever drank any of them. What had happened to their radical views, their desire to implement real revolution, the men of the SA asked?

An early view of the SA at one of their interminable rallies.

Had Hitler betrayed them? History has proved that all too often upheavals in the government or autocracy of a country seem to require a second or even a third revolution within a very short space of time. The movers and the shakers who foment the revolution in the first place are all too often overtaken by wilder and more radical thinkers. If those who are dropped or taken out of the picture are lucky, they are consigned to a footnote in history; if not they are invariably put against a wall and shot.

It happened in England in the 1640s and 1650s once Charles I had been defeated and executed by Cromwell and the forces of Parliament; it happened in France at the end of the eighteenth century when the *sans culottes* rabble worked their way through at least three Republican regimes; it happened in Russia in 1917 when Lenin, Trotsky and the Bolsheviks ousted Kerensky and the original revolutionary government. Why not, then, in Germany?

The causes of the Night of the Long Knives are complicated, specific to the age and to the characteristics of the individuals involved, as we shall see. But, like those second revolutions in England, Russia and France, one element was consistent: the need to eliminate people who had done their job and were now unable to see that they were redundant or out of time. In Germany in 1934 the brutal excision of the men who had helped Hitler to power, men who were suddenly dispensable elements in the wider game, played a vital role in securing the Nazi dictatorship.

Hitler, like the other leading members of the Party, was no democrat. From the beginning his aim was to be a totalitarian dictator. It was, he felt, the only way to rule and run a country like Germany. He was ruthless and violent—but only when he had to be. To Hitler dictatorship did not involve mere brutality; it was the exercise of control by one man, the implementation of one idea. But when and if violence was needed Hitler was well able to use it and use it effectively.

The most tragic part of Hitler managing to secure his dictatorship was that he did not actually seize power; it was handed to him, legally, democratically and in all innocence by those who should have known better. The Night of the Long Knives was just the start of a descent into the darkest night and the most brutal dictatorship Europe had ever seen. And it had happened without Hitler really trying. It was something that no one, with the exception of Adolf Hitler, ever imagined possible. The other members in the top echelon of the Party, clever men like Göring and Goebbels, had not thought that through. They were more interested in personal advancement and scoring victories over possible challengers for a place around Hitler's table.

Not even Ernst Röhm had thought that far ahead. His aims were far more prosaic, in particular his schemes to take over the army. Yet the putsch that destroyed him was

Ernst Röhm, the most thuggish of all the SA thugs.

a seminal moment that decided the fate of Germany and settled the direction of the country for the next fifty years, way beyond the demise of Hitler and the dividing of a conquered Germany into two.

After the Night of the Long Knives, Hitler was effectively in control of Germany for as long as he wanted, or at least until he overreached himself and brought external retribution to bear. Put in those terms the loss of old Party comrades was a sacrifice worth making. The coup, or putsch, call it what you will, was conducted with the utmost violence with no quarter asked or given. Some of the murders were horrific in their violence, bodies being hacked to pieces, bullet after bullet being pumped into already-dead corpses. The occasional firing squad was almost humane by comparison. Friends and colleagues of many years standing were ruthlessly hunted down and eliminated by those with ultimate power. So, too, were old enemies as scores were settled, debts were called in and opportunities for self-aggrandizement suddenly presented themselves. Revenge was real and tangible in the air.

Compared to the later pogroms, witch-hunts and massacres in Nazi Germany the Night of the Long Knives was small beer. But it was the first, the first of many, and it should have told the statesmen of the world exactly what sort of people now held the reins of power in Germany. The fact that it failed to register with most of their self-satisfied, traditionally conservative egos was as much a condemnation of them as it was of the Nazi regime.

Adolf Hitler and Enlistment

Adolf Hitler moved to Munich in 1913, mainly to escape arrest for his avoidance of military service in the Austrian army. Having lived in the Bavarian city for several months he was eventually picked up by the police in early 1914 and sent back to Austria for induction into the Austrian army. However, having lived rough in Vienna and then Munich for some considerable time, he was undersized and a poor physical specimen. As a consequence, when he arrived at Salzburg on 5 February 1914 he failed his medical. He was told, quite clearly, that there would be no Austrian army for him and he was allowed to return to Munich. Hitler was not opposed to being a soldier; he just did not want to be an Austrian soldier, having always been a vocal supporter of the idea of 'greater Germany', and a unification of Germany and Austria. When war broke out in the summer of 1914 he was twenty-five years old and still living in Munich. Always a German patriot, Hitler was more than happy to offer his services to the Bavarian military. It was, he felt, his duty to serve the great German nation.

Enlistment was not a given, however. He was, technically, still an Austrian citizen and therefore had to request permission to serve Germany before

Hitler, seated left, during the Great War.

he could be admitted to the ranks. It would have been a few days of worry and concern for Hitler—would he be allowed to join up, would he be sent back to Austria?—but finally permission was granted without too much fuss.

Hitler was enrolled as a private in the 16th Bavarian Reserve Regiment. It was not long before the unit became known as the List Regiment in honour of the commanding officer, Julius List, who was killed at the first Battle of Ypres in October 1914. Hitler was always proud to have been a member of this elite regiment which fought in most of the Western Front campaigns.

It later transpired that his enlistment in the Bavarian army was actually a mistake by the German authorities. When he failed his medical in February 1914 Hitler should have been deported to Austria. Instead, he was allowed back into Germany and to settle once more in Munich. When it came to enlistment in August 1914 nobody was unduly concerned about his country of origin: getting men to the front was considerably more important. It makes an interesting point: had Hitler been deported in February 1914 or had his attempt to enlist in the Bavarian army in August of the same year failed, what would have become of him? Would he have gone on to serve in the Austrian army, having already avoided service for the country and then been subsequently turned down because of poor health? Both questions are imponderables but one thing is clear: the history of the world would have been quite different.

Hitler in determined mood, under an arch of Brownshirt salutes.

1. SHARPENING THE KNIVES

The moment the Junkers 52 dipped its starboard wing and swung elegantly around for the approach to Oberwisen airfield, Adolf Hitler felt a calmness settle itself within him. Everything from the regular and rhythmical thump of the plane's three engines to the rattle of knives and forks in the galley seemed suddenly familiar and safe. He had been nervous, excited even, since leaving Berlin the previous day. From the capital he had headed south to attend the wedding of a Party official and had spent the night at his usual haunt, the comfortable and welcoming Hotel Dreesen at Godesberg on the banks of the river Rhine. He had never had a bad night there but this time, whatever the comforts of the hotel, Hitler had endured an evening of rain and squalls. For hours the wind had battered at roof and windows like the Valkyries themselves. Fortunately, by midnight it had all gone quiet, leaving the skies above the river clear and ideal for flying.

Fine, that was how it was in Godesberg but what was it like farther west? Hitler spent another couple of restless hours, this time in his bedroom, and was happy when the call came from his pilot to say that the weather over Munich had also cleared. They could now take off. Hurrying by car to his aircraft, Hitler left Hangelar airfield outside Bonn just after 0200 that morning.

The Junkers 52—a plane like this carried Hitler to Munich in 1934.

Of course it had been the perfect strategy, taking those twenty-four hours out of Berlin at what, despite everything, many still thought of as a moment of supreme crisis. If nothing else it would disarm Röhm and the SA leaders. Sitting, now, in the uncomfortable bucket seat of the Junkers, Hitler giggled out loud at the pun: disarm Röhm indeed. Perfect strategy, yes, but the past few months had also been a tense and difficult time. So, too, had that taut and gut-wrenching twenty-four hours away from Berlin. For once the beauty of the Rhine and of Godesberg in particular had been lost on him. Only now, with the urban sprawl of Munich at last beginning to take shape through the early morning mist, could he finally allow himself to enjoy a degree of contentment.

Making the final decision had not been easy; after all Röhm had been a friend and a comrade for many years. Waiting and deciding exactly what to do and when to do it had taken their toll. For months now he had been under pressure, constantly worrying and feeling that he was being pushed into a position where he would have no choice but to make an emotional decision.

They had all been insistent and had kept on at him, Göring, Himmler and the other senior Party members; the army and even the president himself had been constantly putting in their penny ha'pennies as well. Make a decision, they had all said; what they had meant was make the decision we want.

The emotional response would have been to let Röhm off the rope, to send him into exile or banish him to the deepest recesses of the Black Forest. But that would have been no good, Hitler knew, and it would have been only a matter of time before Röhm came back to haunt him, whatever he might promise or swear. Hitler knew his weaknesses, particularly where Ernst was concerned. Despite how angry he felt he knew that there was even the possibility that he might invite his oldest friend back at some stage. No, the hard-edged, realistic option was what was needed. In the end he had resisted making a decision from the heart and now he was glad of it.

He nodded his head and muttered out loud, a habit he had retained from childhood. He rapped harshly on the seat rest with the knuckles of his right hand. "It was the right decision. I know it was."

One of the Schutzstaffel (SS) guards from the back of the aircraft began to move forward, thinking that the Führer had asked for something. Hitler waved him away and stared out of the window.

"Emotion and friendship have no place in politics," he mumbled to himself, stretching out his legs and curling his lip into a snarl. "If things were different Röhm would do exactly the same as me."

He was glad the waiting was over. He had never been good at 'holding fire' but momentum was finally gathering and it was too late now to back down, even had he wanted. He smiled to himself. The great gambler, his Party colleague and deputy

Rudolf Hess had called him, and there was no bigger gamble than this, of that he was sure. So, it was a gamble, yes, but essential if he and the Party were to survive. Survive and grow!

He glanced across the aisle to where his propaganda chief Joseph Goebbels was sitting, hunched up and pretending to stare out of the window at the ground beneath. Already the fields and farms, the forests and lakes were beginning to take shape, seeming to grow like mushrooms out of the darkness. But Hitler knew that Goebbels did not see or notice them. His agile mind would be focused on the day ahead.

Hitler did not fully trust Goebbels and had not been sure which side he would back in the coming showdown. The man seemed to be altogether too willing to bend with the wind. In the beginning he had been a friend and supporter of Gregor Strasser but had switched sides to join Hitler some years ago. All of the Gestapo reports from the surveillance Hitler had asked for and received indicated that Goebbels had now become a Röhm man through and through. Yet he was here, in the plane with him, seemingly supportive, seemingly happy. And that was good. He needed men with intellects like Goebbels. But he still did not trust him.

Joseph Goebbels and his family: none survived the end of the Reich.

"Two minutes, my Führer," Hans Baur called from the cockpit.

Hitler nodded and lifted his arm in acknowledgement. He liked to fly with the door to the cockpit wide open. That way he could see and hear what was happening, even if the earplugs and the leather flying helmet he wore cut out so much of the sound. One day, he told himself, one day we will have quiet aeroplanes; I will see to that.

The Junkers dropped suddenly as it hit an air pocket and Hitler felt his stomach lurch. Over on the western skyline the city of Munich lay untroubled in the early morning light. Smoke from factories and the houses of early risers reached almost lazily into the air. The artist in him could appreciate the torpor and the delicacy of the scene.

Beyond the city, the long narrow surface of Lake Tegernsee glistened like a million shards of broken glass. They would still be sleeping out there in the hotels and guest-houses of Bad Wiesee, dozens of SA men, untroubled and unprepared for what was about to happen. Good, let them sleep while they still could. For some it would be the last blissful rest they would ever enjoy.

Hans Baur knew his business and, as he had promised, within two minutes the wheels of the heavy Junkers aircraft had kissed the landing strip. Baur was solid and reliable, which was why Hitler had chosen him as his personal pilot, one of many carefully selected men and women who worked for him. People who were that close to the leadership had to be reliable, had to be trustworthy and committed. It did not take the greatest intellect in the world to see that Baur was both of these.

As soon as the aircraft had rolled to a stop, Hitler was out of his seat and at the door. It swung open to reveal the tall shape of Erich Kempka, one of the many chauffeurs attached to the Führer's office. Kempka was another loyal and dedicated Party comrade. Behind the chauffeur four black-uniformed SS men stood rigidly to attention. Kempka indicated the low-slung Mercedes that was now parked alongside the aircraft.

Hans Baur, Hitler's personal pilot.

"All ready, my Führer. Dr Dietrich and Obergruppenführer Lutze are waiting for you in the lounge. They say they need a few minutes of your time."

Hitler made no reply but swung round to stare down the length of the aeroplane. Baur and his co-pilot were still sitting in the cockpit.

"A few hours, Baur," Hitler called. "Make yourself comfortable; go home for a while if you feel like it. Prepare for takeoff at 4 p.m. I want to be back in Berlin by midnight."

"Yes, my Führer," Baur said, rising to his feet.

Hitler waved him back down. "As you were, Baur, as you were."

A quick stop to pick up press chief Dietrich and Victor Lutze, the SA leader from Hanover, and Kempka was soon manoeuvring the Mercedes down the autobahn. Behind them half a dozen cars, full of soldiers, SS men, doctors, press reporters and other officials made up a long convoy of vehicles. It was the usual escort of men and machines, normally just a ceremonial necessity. But not today; today was very different.

"You had a good flight, Führer?" asked Lutze suddenly.

Hitler nodded and grunted a reply. The man was boring and without charm but he did at least have the saving grace of being loyal, which was a lot more than could be said for Röhm and his set of debauched followers.

They lapsed into a sullen silence as Kempka ghosted them through the Munich suburbs. Dietrich and Lutze had greeted him with news of another drunken outrage that had taken place only the night before. A gang of brown-shirted SA thugs—or

Erich Kempka drives Hitler—with Mussolini alongside him—in the familiar open-topped tourer so beloved by all Nazi hierarchy.

Stormtroopers as they preferred to call themselves—had run rampant through the city. It was exactly the type of behaviour that the army and the industrialists who were still pumping money into the Nazi coffers hated and despised. It was yet another reason why something had to be done about Röhm's private little army.

Little, Hitler thought? It was hardly little. He pushed back his hair and fingered the leather whip he always kept stored in the Mercedes. At the last count there were over three million Stormtroopers in the country. They had been useful in the Nazi climb to power, ideal for the brawling battles that had claimed the streets for the Party. The brown-shirted, jackbooted SA had done their job most effectively but now their usefulness had passed. Hadn't it? He pushed away the sliver of doubt and told himself once again that, yes, this was the right decision.

In a screech of tyres, Hitler's car pulled into the forecourt of the Bavarian interior ministry. He was out of the vehicle and halfway up the steps before his bodyguard from the car behind managed to catch up with him.

The dozen or so guilty SA men were gathered together in a room on the top floor, shamefaced now and clearly worried. It was so easy, Hitler thought. He screamed at them, ranting and raving, spittle flying from his lips, and they cowered away.

SA police chief Schneidhuber, one of the first victims of the Night of the Long Knives.

It was, as he later told himself, a good performance.

"You are scum," he roared, "all of you, a disgrace to the uniforms you wear. Well, no longer."

He turned to the SS guards who had followed him up the stairs. "Lock them up. I can't be bothered to deal with swine like that today. They're tomorrow's problem."

How easy it was. Everybody, Dietrich and Lutze included, thought he was out of control, thought that his famous temper had boiled over. But inside he was as cold as ice. Acting and politics, he knew, went together so well.

A few minutes more to humiliate the local police chief, Obergruppenführer Schneidhuber, Hitler reckoned and then he could get on with the real business of the day. He swung round to face the worried official. "You," Hitler screamed, "are as bad as the rest of them. You are supposed to keep them in check!"

"But Führer, how can I ..."

"How can you what? Control them? Find a way, you fool."

The police chief looked as if he might cry.

"Schneidhuber, you're a traitor, a bloody traitor!"

He leapt forward and seized the man by the front of his shirt. The look of sheer terror on August Schneidhuber's face was so reassuring, Hitler thought. He was pleased that despite the last few months of cabinet meetings and discussions, dinner parties and the best hotels—the soft life as he liked to call it—he had not lost his touch. It was difficult to prevent a smile from creeping into his eyes as he ripped the Nazi badges and insignia from Schneidhuber's uniform.

"Get out of my sight," Hitler hissed, thrusting the man away, hurling him to one side and then watching as he was led off to the cells. He did not know but he would guess that the local SS would be more than happy to accommodate the police chief.

Hitler stood for a moment, sneering, inhaling deeply and ensuring that his breathing was right before appearing again downstairs in front of the Party officials and members of the SS. He glared at the gathered men with contempt, his cold hard eyes sweeping over the assembly. Then he turned on his heel and went out of the door, closely followed by his guards. It had been one of his better performances but it had only been the overture, the beginning. Now it was time for the main performance, time for the Hotel Hanselbauer and for Ernst Röhm.

*

Operation Hummingbird it was called and, no doubt about it, from beginning to end its execution was stunningly effective. Hitler was delighted. The shock of sudden fear, the panic as cold hands pulled them violently from their beds and sleep, meant that the capture and arrest of Ernst Röhm and the SA leaders went off without a hitch.

Half-awake, half-dressed, most of them did not understand what was happening or why. And for those who were more aware, none of them could believe that this was being done to them by the Führer, the man to whom they had pledged their lives and honour. Without ceremony they were pushed and pulled into the hotel's laundry room or into the cellar, isolated places where SS guards ensured they would stay, well away from the rest of the building.

Hitler himself was at the forefront of the operation, brandishing his whip in one hand, a pistol in the other as he charged up the stairs and into Röhm's bedroom. Smashing open the door Hitler screamed at his former friend, "Röhm, you are under arrest."

Röhm was alone but as the bedroom door crashed open his personal physician and wife suddenly emerged from an ante room. It has never been clear what they were

The Hotel Hanselbauer, now demolished, was the scene of the first arrests.

doing there—plotting, planning, treating Röhm for some ailment? It hardly mattered. They were small players of little or no consequence.

Lutze spoke up for them, however, and Hitler, now almost inexplicably full of dignity and human kindness, shook the doctor's hand and advised the pair to leave quietly. The Hotel Hanselbauer, he explained, would not be the place to see or be seen in for the next few hours.

Röhm, the scarred, pug-nasty SA brawler sat silently drinking coffee, as if he had already accepted his fate. He might seem unperturbed but inside his emotions would have been whirling. Not least would have been the thought that the Führer, his friend and companion of many years, had betrayed him. He would never have thought it possible. Erich Kempka, the chauffeur, later gave an account of Röhm's last few minutes as a free man: "Now the bus arrives. Quickly, the SA leaders are collected from the laundry room and walk past Röhm under police guard. Röhm looks up from his coffee sadly and waves to them in a melancholy way. At last, Röhm too is led from the hotel. He walks past Hitler with his head bowed, completely apathetic."

In the room next to the SA commander's, Röhm's deputy, Edmund Heines, had been found in bed with a young Stormtrooper, confirmation—if any was needed—of the debauchery that was rife within the SA organization. Hitler and Goebbels could not hide their contempt.

Heines, a giant of a man with the face of an angel, tried to resist. It was a passive performance; he refused to get out of bed and Hitler told him that he had five minutes to rise, dress and be ready to leave. The alternative was to be shot where he lay. But when the five minutes had elapsed Heines was still sprawled naked in his bed, almost as if he didn't care about the Führer or his commands. Hitler called for the SS and they dragged the recalcitrant Heines and his eighteen-year-old lover from the bed. They threw some clothes at the pair and hustled them away.

According to some sources Heines, along with his companion, was manhandled to the road outside, made to kneel on the tarmac and shot; other accounts say that, like most of the SA men, he was taken to Stadelheim prison and was executed there.

Edmund Heines, Röhm's deputy, another early victim of the purge.

Throughout the morning senior SA officers kept arriving at the Munich railway station. These were men who, due to the lateness of the summons, had not been able to leave their posts the night before. Now they were arrested the moment they set foot on the platform.

Many were locked up in Stadelheim and other prisons, many more were summarily executed, without even the farce of a mock trial. By midday Hitler had broken the back of any resistance or plan that Röhm may have harboured to mount his own, second revolution. As he gloatingly declared to thousands of cheering adherents at the Party rally a few months later: "During the next thousand years no more revolutions will take place in Germany."

The danger was over almost before it had begun, and yet, for a while, the arrests continued unabated. In Berlin, in Munich, anywhere where SA leaders were felt to be particular supporters of Röhm, the police and the SS continued their visitations It was only on 2 July, three days after the arrest of Röhm, that Hitler finally called an end to the arrests and the killings.

Inevitably, within hours news of the purge had leaked out to foreign newspapers and officials. As well as the indefatigable Reuters News Agency, all newspapers kept correspondents in Germany and it was impossible to keep the story—even if it was only a story of half-truths and fabrications—either secret or hidden.

The grim and forbidding walls of the Stadelheim prison where many of the SA met their ends.

The German public, however? Well that was a somewhat different matter and it was felt better to keep the scale of the operation hidden from them, for the time being at least.

On 10 July, over a week after the arrests, Nazi propaganda chief Joseph Goebbels stood up in front of an audience and made the first formal acknowledgement of Operation Hummingbird.

Emphasizing the point—more fiction than fact—that Röhm had been about to launch a putsch against the legally elected government of Germany, he praised Hitler for having had the courage to act immediately and with vigour. The bravery of the Führer was beyond doubt, Goebbels declared. He had put his own life in danger in order to safeguard the people of Germany. For months or years even, people had been screaming about the debauched and violent behaviour of the Stormtroopers. Well, now Hitler had done something about it.

In his speech Goebbels also thanked the German media for their restraint which had kept the German public more or less unaware of the operation but criticized foreign newspapers for their false reporting of events.

Hitler's first acknowledgement of the arrests came in a speech he gave on 13 July. Defending his actions and setting out reasons why he had taken justice into his own hands, the Führer also gave the purge its popular name—the Night of the Long

Knives. The Night of the Long Knives was a phrase from a Nazi song of the time. It was a theatrical term, engaging and even a little romantic. There was nothing even faintly romantic about Hitler's pogrom, however, even though the terminology was misleading and cloaked three days of bloody murder.

The Night of the Long Knives; it gave the faintest hint of respectability to the arrests and assassinations and was a phrase which perfectly suited the events of the early summer in 1934.

No matter how well it was all covered or explained and in spite of the terminology employed, the culling of the SA was a dramatic and brutal affair which left at least eighty-four dead—some claims a death toll of over 400, some nearer a thousand. So many personal vendettas were settled that the true figure will never be really known.

But in order to fully understand how and why such a mass killing was deemed necessary we have to go back to the beginnings of the Nazi Party, to the wild and distressing days after the end of the Great War. In those long-gone days of excitement and expectation lie the origins of the massacre—and, indeed, of the Nazi Party itself.

Hitler and the Great War

Having enlisted in the 16th Bavarian Reserve Regiment—the List Regiment as it was known throughout the German army—Hitler served honourably and bravely for the duration of the Great War. His introduction to combat was as an infantryman at the First Battle of Ypres in October 1914. In Germany the battle is still known as the 'Massacre of the Innocents' as the German army suffered 40,000 casualties, mostly from the newly enlisted volunteers, in just three weeks. The List Regiment came out of combat with 611 survivors, one of whom was Adolf Hitler.

In the wake of the battle Hitler was promoted to *gefreiter* (lance-corporal). He never climbed higher up the ranks because, it was said, he lacked leadership ability. At that stage in his life Hitler really did not mind. It was after Ypres that Hitler became a runner, taking messages across the battlefield and back to headquarters. It was a role that suited him. Never the most gregarious of soldiers, he deplored the usual smutty talk of infantrymen in the trenches and invariably preferred to be alone with his thoughts and dreams. His companions did not really know what to make of him. He didn't swear or, like the rest of them, tell dirty jokes. And he did not drink or smoke, which was useful as he traded his regular issue of tobacco for their tins of jam; but was still accepted enough to earn the nickname of Adi. He adopted a small stray dog, *Fuchsl* or Little Fox, as Hitler called him, training the animal to perform tricks and become a much-loved companion. In 1917, when the List Regiment was in the process of transferring to a quieter part of the line in the Alsace, Fuchsl and Hitler's portfolio of sketches went missing. It was presumed that they had been stolen by a soldier who was never found out or punished. Hitler was devastated.

The List Regiment fought in most of the great campaigns of the war, including the battle of the Somme, where Hitler received a wound in the thigh when a shell exploded close by. He spent two months in a Red Cross hospital before returning to his unit. He also took an eighteen-day leave, spending it in Berlin with the family of one of his comrades.

He won the Iron Cross Second Class in 1914 and then, in 1918, he earned the far more prestigious Iron Cross First Class. Rarely given to a non-commissioned officer, Hitler was recommended for the decoration by Lieutenant Hugo Guttmann, the regiment's Jewish adjutant.

When the Armistice was signed in November 1918 Hitler was in hospital, having been temporarily blinded in a British mustard gas attack. He was devastated but had already adopted the right-wing anti-Semitic attitudes that had begun to infiltrate the military in those final days of the war. Distraught, feeling that the world had ended, it was those attitudes that helped give him a goal and a plan for the future.

Hitler, seated right, during the Great War.

2. AN END OF WAR

Nobody expected the Great War to end on 11 November 1918. The German armies were in retreat but they were not beaten and no invader's foot had cast so much as a shadow onto the soil of the Fatherland when the Armistice was signed that autumn morning in a railway carriage in the Compiègne forest. Back in Germany, there had been revolutionary outbreaks, mutinies and demonstrations by sailors and by disgruntled civilians in Kiel and Berlin. The uprisings might have been the thin end of the wedge, the beginning of the end for the Kaiser's empire, but they were uncomfortably similar to the previous year's events in Russia. News of the rebellions came as a shock, not just to the Kaiser and to the public, but particularly to the soldiers still serving at the front. For men who had fought for four long years and would continue to fight as long as resistance was required, it was like a hammer blow to the back of the skull.

For Corporal Adolf Hitler, in hospital, temporarily isolated and sealed into a world of darkness due to the effect of a recent gas attack, the metaphor of a shadowy and

The Armistice is signed; an artist's impression of the German surrender in November 1918.

bottomless pit was hard to resist. His whole world had tumbled into blackness and he was left with a feeling of despair that matched his physical ailments. Everything he believed in or hoped for had been smashed away. And yet, in a way, Hitler was lucky. He could do something about his injuries—or rather time and the efforts of his doctors and nurses could do it for him—and he could also try to do something about the state of Germany. It might take longer to repair Germany than it would to make him see again but almost from the moment he was released from hospital he had an aim in life. It was a single and all-consuming mission: to make Germany great again.

Hitler was discharged into a world that was markedly different from anything he had known before. To begin with the Kaiser had gone. In the wake of the autumn revolutions the emperor had been told that his army might well continue to serve Germany but certainly not him. Kaiser Wilhelm had no option but to abdicate and immediately went to Holland where he lived for the rest of his life as an exile. In the wake of his withdrawal a Social Democratic Republican government had been established in Berlin.

The task of easing an exhausted and demoralized Germany out of the war had fallen to this new Socialist Republican government. Significantly, the Armistice had been signed for Germany by Matthias Erzberger, a Jewish politician who with one stroke of the pen gave Hitler and the future Nazi Party all the anti-Semitic propaganda they needed. Erzberger knew the risks but as a patriot and as a pragmatic politician, in November 1918 there was nothing else that he could have done.

Right-wing factions, represented by generals such as Ludendorff and Hindenburg, never accepted the surrender. They did not, could not, acknowledge the fact that Germany was on her knees, that the population was a mere few weeks away from starvation and that the nation's armies were just about tottering on the edge of a sheer precipice. They held firmly to the fallacy that German forces had never been beaten and, as a by-product of that belief, the right-wing politicians and their supporters were instrumental in creating the two myths that were much bandied about in Germany for the next twenty-five years. These were the beliefs or talismans that all German Nationalists clung to as a shipwrecked sailor might cling to a life raft—that of the "November criminals" and the stab in the back. The myths were something of a double-edged sword, as A. N. Wilson has described them: "The Social Democrats, egged on by Communists and Jews, had drawn Germany into a humiliation from which radical right-wing despotism could alone save it."

In that short sentence not only the culprits but also the cure and the curse of the Weimar Republic were outlined, albeit from a right-wing, conservative perspective. The culprits, of course, were the Socialists and Jews who had criminally betrayed the German soldiers by signing a peace treaty which had not been needed.

Above: One of Krupp's vast armament factories, seen here in 1915. Hitler relied heavily on their support in his rise to power.

Right: The Spartacist uprising was one of the more serious outbreaks of violence against Germany's new socialist republic.

And the solution or the cure came in the shape of the right-wing factions which alone had the courage to stand up for the rights of the German people. The curse lay in the fact that a large number of the German people swallowed the lie implicitly.

The result of the Armistice was confusion and anarchy with the ten months from November 1918 to August 1919 marking a revolutionary period in German history. It was a time of gun battles and riots and, in particular, events like a general strike and the Spartacist uprising of January 1919.

The communist Spartacists, under the leadership of Rosa Luxemburg and Karl Liebknecht, held Berlin and many parts of Germany in thrall for several weeks with blood and corpses a common enough sight on the streets of German cities. Hitler and other right-wing supporters were in despair until events came to a head.

The new president of the republic, Friedrich Ebert, finally decided that such lawlessness could not continue and threw in armed Freikorps troops; the Spartacists were crushed, Luxemburg and Liebknecht captured and beaten unconscious by the rifle butts of their captors. Then they were shot in the head. Rosa's body was dumped into the Landwehr canal; Karl Liebknecht's delivered, unannounced, to a city morgue

Rosa Luxemburg, one of the Spartacist leaders. She was murdered by the Freikorps troops that were sent in to put down the rebellion.

The roaming menace of the right-wing Freikorps, bands of ex-soldiers dedicated to destroying all communist opposition, was not something that would go away quickly or easily. They might have destroyed the Spartacists but over the coming years the Freikorps themselves went on to create more violence and terror. In Hitler's Munich there was even a communist coup d'état which was supported by the army—Hitler included—and which held power until right-wing forces moved in to destroy them.

The Treaty of Versailles, signed in the summer of 1919, might have brought this period of uncertainty to a close but the Treaty was a disaster for Germany. In the end it solved nothing; in fact it caused considerably more harm than good.

There were no German representatives in the discussions with the result that a vindictive peace settlement was agreed

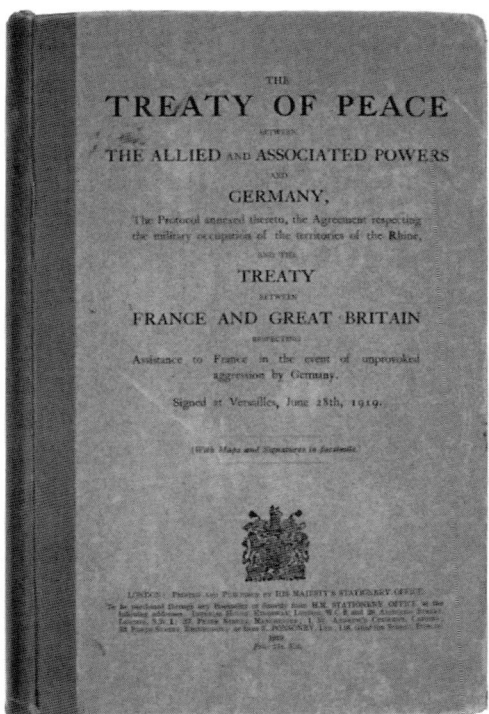

Right: The Treaty of Versailles, 1919.

Below: By the terms of the Treaty of Versailles heavy guns were denied to the German military. This shows workers dismantling an army guns.

and presented, as a fait accompli, to the new republic. There was no opportunity for debate or objection, Allied leaders being adamant that Germany was to be so crushed underfoot that she would never again rise to any position of power.

The German army, air force and navy had already been reduced to impotence or, as in the case of the air force, totally destroyed. Germany could not have resisted in any way and representatives of the Weimar Republic, the 'November criminals' as they were already being called, had no option but to sign the Treaty. The terms were brutal and, in the words of Harriet Wood, virtually guaranteed a further worldwide conflict within a relatively short space of time: "Germany lost one-eighth of her land area in Europe, including valuable mineral resources and six and a half million people. Her overseas colonies were confiscated."

Perhaps most galling of all, the War Guilt Clause of the Treaty laid all blame for the conflict on Germany which was ordered to pay enormous reparations, in the region of $32 billion, to the victorious allies. It was a shattering burden to place on the crippled economy of a country that was already reeling from the emotional consequences of defeat.

Into this world of chaos and confusion stepped Adolf Hitler. He was ideal 'Freikorps fodder' but, to begin with, he remained within the army. It would be stretching things to call him a spy but for a few months he was one of several soldiers and former

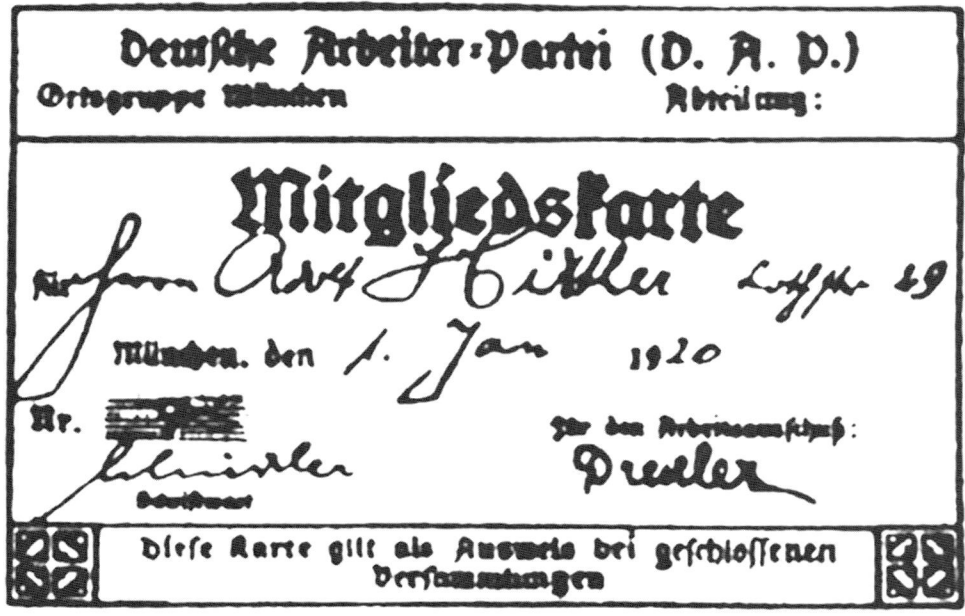

Hitler's membership card for the German Workers' Party.

soldiers monitoring the activities of potential revolutionary groups in the Munich area. As part of his duties Hitler had to attend and report on lectures, meetings and rallies organized by what were really fringe groups in the Bavarian political scene. Hitler made his reports, as ordered, but he also had another, personal agenda. Outspoken, driven and with a clear vision of what Germany needed, he was seeking like-minded individuals that he could work with and use.

With this in mind, in 1919 he almost stumbled across the German Workers' Party, a tiny, inconsequential group whose political stance was about as far right as you could get. It was exactly what he wanted: obscure, effectively leaderless—despite the honest but ineffective efforts of its founder Anton Drexler—and unclear which direction it should take. It was the ideal organization, a vehicle, rather than a ready-made political structure, for someone like Hitler to grab and mould to his own ends.

The story of how Hitler achieved this is well known and does not require repeating here. Suffice to say that he joined the German Workers' Party as member No. 7, discovered that he had a talent in oratory and within a year was addressing meetings of over five or six hundred rowdy listeners in the beer halls that served as the epicentres of Munich politics in those days.

Soon acclaimed as a notable public speaker, this postcard shows Hitler addressing a political meeting. With him are Herman Göring and Julius Streicher.

He became part of the organizing committee of the Party and was soon a well-known figure on the Bavarian political scene. It was hardly a national image or agenda but it was a start. Leaving the army in 1920, he decided to devote his life to politics becoming, first, the mouthpiece and figurehead of the German Workers' Party and then its leader.

After events like the Spartacist uprising and the brief period of communist control in Munich, the world of post-war German politics continued to be violent and brutal. Organizations that had the physical strength to survive, to bully other agencies off the political stage, were often more important than any message they might carry or try to impart. Hitler needed supporters who were as ruthless as him and, from this early stage, began to gather about him men who would offer unswerving loyalty and would stay with him to the end.

Dedicated Nazis like Rudolf Hess, Alfred Rosenberg, Julius Streicher and Hermann Göring all joined the Party in the early 1920s. There were other less-well-known members of Hitler's inner circle, men like the rough, uncouth Max Amann who became the Party's first business manager, butcher's apprentice Ulrich Graf who acted as

All forms of modern transport were used by Hitler, from aircraft and trains to automobiles. This shows the Nazi leader in one of his cars.

Hitler's bodyguard, and the photographer Heinrich Hoffmann. They came, in the main, from the more unsavoury and fringe elements of the Munich political scene.

One of the early supporters, both of Hitler and of the nascent Nazi Party, was Captain Ernst Röhm, a man who openly admitted his fondness for violence. While he held many of the same bigoted views as Adolf Hitler—in particular a virulent hatred of the Jews, of communism and of democracy—he was also consumed by the desire for perpetual revolution and, as a consequence, by the opportunity such hatred presented for mindless thuggery and violence. Röhm had actually joined the Party before Hitler and, as a member of that rare breed in Germany, an officer who came from the lower middle class rather than the usual aristocratic background, he was of real value to the early Nazi Party. He had contacts in the military and he had experience of both traditional warfare and of the squalid but equally vicious battles on the streets.

Despite his background and stated belief in socialism Röhm was also dedicated to Nationalism and to the destruction of the Weimar Republic. Importantly, he was able to tap into that element of society which quickly became essential for Nazi success—the thousands of unemployed, dissatisfied ex-soldiers who were looking for a leader, even a messiah. Like several of the early Nazi leaders Röhm was a homosexual and did nothing to hide the fact. It has never been totally clear whether Hitler himself had homosexual tendencies—he certainly had some bizarre sexual fetishes—but at that early stage Röhm's predilections did not appear to hinder or hurt their relationship.

Röhm, quickly understanding what Hitler wanted, was able to bring countless numbers of disaffected young men into the Party. By and large they were recently discharged soldiers like him, dejected and unhappy after the Treaty of Versailles, men who felt rootless after four years of bloody warfare. Violence was almost a way of life for them and, as Röhm assured these newcomers, they would get their share of it in the political meetings and marches that the Party organized.

They joined in droves, hugely expanding the membership, and, once enrolled as members of the SA, they became part of the largest paramilitary organization the country had ever seen. Offered the chance of structure, comradeship and sense of

Public meetings during the Weimar Republic were often huge affairs. This shows a meeting being held, as they often were, in one of Munich's many beer halls.

purpose, they eagerly swore loyalty to the two most important people in their lives, Adolf Hitler and Ernst Röhm. The initial success of the Nazi street fighters can be found in that dual hero worship but it also sowed the future seeds of unrest. Two autocrats or tyrants cannot easily co-exist within the same organization, as the Roman Empire discovered after the death of Julius Caesar in the first century AD. One will invariably emerge as the true leader; the other will be consigned to ignominy and even death. For the moment, though, both Hitler and Röhm seemed to be happy enough. Together, they oversaw the introduction of Hitler's twenty-five-point manifesto, the changing of the Party's name to the National Socialist German Workers' Party and the organization of the strong-arm squads—used, initially to protect Nazi speakers and disrupt other party events—into something resembling a military force.

As with any emerging or developing group, there were minor altercations within the organization and in the autumn of 1921 an attempt by Anton Drexler, the original founder and leader of the Party, to undermine Hitler was easily seen off when the future dictator threatened to resign. The National Socialist Party without Hitler was something that Drexler knew they could ill afford. The well-meaning but ineffectual locksmith who had given Hitler his first chance of political success bowed to the inevitable and faded from the scene.

By the summer of 1923, however, there was pressure of a different sort, this time from Röhm and his SA thugs. By the autumn it was intense. They wanted more than just street fights; they wanted power and riches. With the German economy looking ever more brittle Hitler knew that if he did not do something significant or make some grand gesture of defiance, his days as Party leader would soon be over. He decided to gamble and launch an armed uprising that might just catapult him to the leadership of Bavaria.

The Beer Hall Putsch took place on 8 November 1923. It began when Hitler, Göring and twenty-five SA men burst into the Burgerbraukeller where Gustav von Kahr and others were holding a political meeting. Hitler fired a pistol shot into the ceiling and proclaimed that the revolution had begun.

The SA immediately set up a cordon around the building and no one was allowed to leave. Meanwhile Hitler took the three speakers, General von Lessow, Colonel von Seisser and Gustav von Kahr, the latter being effectively the leader or prime minister of Bavaria, into an ante room to thrash out the details of the new regime.

The Great War hero General Eric Ludendorff was added to the mix when he arrived, later than expected, at the beer hall. He had been courted by the Nazis but was not entirely enthusiastic, rather looking down his nose at Hitler and his organization. Even so he had told the Nazis he would be there and, despising the liberal Left, was quite willing to see what might happen.

Above: Nazi troops wait for their orders during the Beer Hall putsch of 1923.

Below: Gustav von Kahr, Bavarian leader, talks with General Ludendorff.

The story of the putsch is one of ineptitude, double-dealing and broken pledges. Kahr, in particular, quickly reneged on his promise to support the revolution. It was something that, as far as Hitler and the Nazis were concerned, was unforgivable and marked the old politician down for eventual retribution.

The putsch ended with armed police firing on a large marching column of Nazis. Sixteen Nazis and two police were killed, many more wounded. Only Ludendorff emerged with any dignity, walking calmly through a hail of police bullets, while Hitler, Röhm and others fell to the ground and were arrested. Sentenced by a sympathetic judge to just five years' imprisonment, Hitler was out of gaol before he had served a year and immediately set about rebuilding his shattered Party.

If the failed putsch had taught Hitler one thing it was simply that the way to power lay through the ballot box. Street thugs were useful, necessary even, but they were no use at all when pitched against the full force of government and political respectability. For the Nazi Party to obtain ultimate power in Germany it would have to begin with the legal process of election. Only the due process of democracy would allow them into a position where the German populace would accept them as a serious political enterprise. That was the future, Hitler knew, but it was a decision that was bound to create conflict with people like Röhm.

During his time in prison another new star—or, as Hitler saw it, another rival—had risen within the ranks of the Party, Gregor Strasser. Like Röhm, Strasser was interested in the promised socialist values of National Socialism. He was a good organizer and was one of thirty-two Nazi-orientated Reichstag deputies. Almost on principal, Hitler hated and distrusted him.

The relaunch of the Nazi Party on 27 February 1925 was a watershed. It marked the move toward some sort of respectability and that, for people like Ernst Röhm, was of little interest. Over the next few months, Röhm quarrelled and then broke with Hitler before taking ship to South America. Once there he became a lieutenant-colonel in the Bolivian army, a role that for a while at least more than fulfilled his desire for violence.

Gregor Strasser was Hitler's rival for leadership of the Nazi Party.

Röhm's departure for Bolivia coincided with the death of President Ebert. In his place Field Marshal Paul von Hindenburg, hero of the Great War, reluctantly agreed to step into the role. As he put it, he would serve for the good of the Fatherland. In his self-imposed South American exile Röhm noted the appointment and despite Hindenburg's age thought that it would be good for the country.

However, Hitler and the Nazi Party had not finished with Ernst Röhm. He had left the SA and the now leaderless Stormtroopers behind him when he went off to Bolivia. Large numbers of armed ruffians were useful to Hitler but, unless they were marshalled and directed, they could also prove very dangerous. By 1930 the SA was almost beyond control and Hitler appealed to Röhm to return, take command of the SA and reduce the amount of violence on the streets.

Röhm agreed and booked a return passage to Germany. Once installed as the chief of staff of the SA, he began putting the house in order and, in the process, building himself a solid power base within the Nazi Party. Hitler noted this "party within the party" but, for the moment, he needed the SA and had no option other than to accept the situation.

In those post-prison years Gregor Strasser, along with his brother Otto and a new recruit by the name of Joseph Goebbels, were making a more than effective fist of organizing the northern elements of the Nazi Party. There was for a while even the possibility of Hitler being superseded as leader. The Berlin element was strong but in the end it came to nothing, Hitler's charm or charisma winning Goebbels over to his side and effectively sidelining the Strasser brothers.

After the Wall Street Crash and the destabilizing of the world economy, support for Hitler and the Nazis grew rapidly. Unemployment and inflation meant disaster for many political parties but not for the Nazis. For them it was the ideal breeding ground for success and, of course, they had one extra arrow to their bow: "Economic troubles compelled the people to favour right-wing solutions, and in the disastrous days of the early 1930s, Hitler's anti-Semitism was an attractive feature to many German voters. The Jews formed an identifiable and useful scapegoat against whom to direct the rage, frustration, fear and misery that ordinary Germans had experienced for nearly half a generation."[*]

The Jews were an easy target. Numbering less than one percent of the entire German population they were easily identified as being 'different' and were marked down as the ideal people to take the rap for so many of Germany's problems.

In keeping with Hitler's notions of the legal road to power the Nazi Party fought in each one of the elections that marked the late 1920s and early 1930s. There were a plethora of them, all contested in the usual manner of speeches, posters and marches, albeit with the SA continuing to browbeat and bully opponents.

---

[*]   Charles Rivers Editions

A Goebbels-inspired anti-Semitic poster: "When you see this sign [Star of David]".

Symptomatic of the uncertain times, it sometimes seemed as if there was an election every other month. None of the elected parties and governments ever managed to provide the solution to Germany's problems but slowly and surely the National Socialists grew in size and power. As they gained more seats in the Reichstag and with so many other parties failing to provide any answer to the economic woes of the country, to many of the more gullible observers it seemed as if the Nazis were the only people with any notion about how to climb out of the mess. Unfortunately for the German people, the Nazis cared a lot more about message than about ideas.

And the Nazi message was simple even if it had little substance. Vote for us and we will create jobs and prosperity, the Party speakers and posters thundered, all the while neglecting to say quite how this miracle would be achieved. The electorate was happy to delude itself, to embrace Hitler's rhetoric and turn away from the beatings and the street battles so enjoyed by the members of the SA, pretending almost that they did not happen.

As the months went on more and more people proved willing to listen to Hitler's ranting speeches. There was only one message: he would make Germany great again. He still

Ernst 'Putzi' Hanfstaengl, one of the early influential supporters of the Nazis, Adolf Hitler and Herman Göring.

ADOLF HITLER

Photography was important to the success of the Nazi Party, images of Hitler in a variety of clothes and uniforms inundating the country. This shows the leader in traditional Bavarian lederhosen.

failed to say how he would do this. In fact he did not know and did not care anyway. The slogans and the street chants were far more important than the political end-product. Understanding stopped at making Germany into a great power once more, an aim and an ideal that everyone in the country wanted to see.

Hitler finally came to power at the end of January 1933 when President Hindenburg, by now over eighty years old, ailing and senile, appointed him to the post of Reich chancellor. It had been a long and rocky road and up to the moment of his appointment Hitler's elevation to the Chancellery had been uncertain. With the Nazis as the largest party in the Reichstag and with administration after administration failing to offer any way out of the economic crisis, there had been, for many months, a heavy groundswell of popular opinion in favour of Adolf Hitler. He should, many thought, be given a chance to put his ideas into practice. It was a view that while being widely held in many middle- and working-class quarters, was something that most of those in the establishment, who saw only the thugs of the SA at work, could not support. That was unfortunate for Hitler as it meant that he and his Party were overlooked for high office time and time again. It stemmed from Hindenburg, of course, the old president regarding Hitler—the 'Bavarian corporal' as he called him –and his supporters, the SA and SS in particular, as mere thugs and criminals.

The Weimar government, despite its socialist leanings, was rooted in the conservatism of old pre-war Germany and had been established in a linear fashion with the post of president at the top of the tree. Beneath the president came the chancellor, the man who effectively ran the country, followed by the members of the cabinet and, finally, the Reichstag or parliament. It was a traditional and rigid system that Hitler was later to abolish, blending the presidency with the chancellorship, but in 1933 the post of chancellor remained the gift of the president.

Throughout the last week of January 1933 there were wild rumours of a projected putsch by the Nazis, a putsch by the army, a general strike and, bizarrely, even an alliance between the trade unions and the military. The waters were made considerably muddier when on Saturday 28 January Hindenburg suddenly and unexpectedly dismissed Chancellor Kurt von Schleicher.

Von Schleicher, like many of the older statesmen who had come of political age during the Kaiser's final years on the throne, was nothing if not a devotee of Machiavelli. He might later claim that he had been repeatedly betrayed during the fifty-seven days he was in office—the shortest serving chancellor in the history of the Weimar Republic—but he was not above plotting and planning himself.

After failing to get Hitler to join him in government, Schleicher immediately attempted to split the Nazi Party. His technique was simple: he would offer Gregor Strasser the post of vice-chancellor in his administration. It was not a bad move.

Convinced that the Party had come to something of a dead halt—it had lost 40 percent of the vote in recent local elections in Thuringia—Gregor Strasser felt

Above left: Field Marshal von Hindenburg, president of the Weimar Republic.

Above right: Kurt von Schleicher, one-time chancellor and soon-to-be victim.

that Hitler had outlived his usefulness. For the sake of the Party and for Germany, he thought, Hitler should now do the decent thing and resign. Hitler, of course, had no intention of retiring from office. It was a misjudgement on Strasser's part but, nevertheless, he turned down von Schleicher's offer.

If he expected thanks or gratitude from the Führer, Gregor Strasser was gravely mistaken. After a bitter row with his leader he resigned from the Party and headed off for a vacation in Italy. Goebbels called him "a dead man" but Hitler was clear—not quite yet.

For all his wheeling and dealing, von Schleicher's fifty-seven days of power had brought no respite for the German people. In fact the mood in the capital was worse than ever and with the trade unions and the big businessmen of the country violently opposed to any form of cooperation with the chancellor—the ex-chancellor as he was soon to become—Hindenburg had no option but to let him go.

Who to turn to now was the president's immediate problem. His initial reaction was to look yet again to a previous holder of the post, the deeply conservative Franz von Papen, but that was a blind alley and even von Papen himself felt that it would be a backward step.

No matter how much the president might hate it, by now there was only one realistic or workable option. There was no real alternative and, begrudging it with every

ounce of his dying soul, Hindenburg was forced to turn to Hitler and his band of fanatics. There would be limitations, however. Hindenburg did not have it in him to hand total control of the government and the country to Hitler and his rabble. Therefore, this would be something of a coalition government.

Turning to Papen, everyone thought, would have been a dreadful mistake but in the end the course of action that Hindenburg chose was to prove equally misjudged. It was also a far more dangerous solution to the social and economic problems of the country, based on the mistaken assumption that he and other establishment figures could actually control Hitler.

Von Papen, the man they all thought could control Hitler.

Hindenburg's idea was to keep the Nazis from a position of real power by granting them some limited degree of control and authority. Yes, Hitler would become chancellor but that, really, was the limit of Hindenburg's gift. The old field marshal had the rather naïve, ludicrous and totally misguided belief that the established politicians, men like von Papen, would be able to manage someone who had half a million paramilitaries at his beck and call.

Hitler might have assumed the top position as chancellor but with the makeup of the government still, for the moment at least, in the hands of the president, the Nazis were given only two offices of state—Wilhelm Frick as minister of the interior and Hitler as Reich chancellor. Von Papen was to be Hitler's vice-chancellor, a shadowy figure of compromise and control within the government. Hitler felt that he could, for the time being at least, work with the situation. He might resent or disagree with Hindenburg's decision but if he wanted power this was how it was going to be.

Von Papen's role was to keep a check on some of the more fanciful notions of the Nazis, preventing them from running riot. It was a role that the wily and vastly experienced von Papen, grateful to be given a part to play in the new order, happily accepted and was confident he could carry out. It was a terrible misjudgement but it was not something that was confined to von Papen. It was a mistake that many would make before realizing that Hitler was not your usual class or type of politician. This was a man for whom lying and cheating were a way of life. However, for the moment at least, von Papen, Hindenburg and the rest felt that they had the measure of the man. The conservatives in his cabinet would control him.

It was a forlorn hope. Von Papen might have brought a degree of respectability to what, really, was still a fringe organization, a party of street brawlers and rabble-rousing tub-thumpers but he was unprepared for the ruthlessness of men like Hitler, Göring and Röhm. The sheer strength of the Nazi following and the spectacle they brought to German politics astounded him.

On the night of Hitler's appointment thousands of torch-bearing Stormtroopers marched through the streets of Berlin in triumph. The combination of darkness and the river of lighted torches flowing down the Under den Linden, the flames guttering like shards of lightning in the wind, were mesmeric. Papen had never seen anything quite like it.

One estimate put the number of marching Stormtroopers at 50,000; another view was that there were less than a quarter of that number available on the night and that the SA Brownshirts simply doubled round the block and appeared in front of Hitler several times.

Either way—and both scenarios are entirely possible—it was an amazing spectacle for those who stood and watched. The determination of the old politician must have

Success at last! Hitler addresses the adoring crowds on the night of his elevation to the chancellorship, January 1933.

quailed at that point. What Hindenburg thought or felt has not been recorded. And von Papen? Increasingly ignored and marginalized, he was soon outclassed by Hindenburg's 'Bavarian corporal' and in the Night of the Long Knives was lucky to escape with his life.

Hitler and von Papen were both ambitious men with a clear view of Germany and her destiny but the difference between the two was simple: one was a gentleman, the other a sadistic psychopath. One had a sense of duty and honour, the other was driven by self-interest and hate. The fact that he survived not just the purge but also the Third Reich in its entirety, only to stand trial at Nuremberg—which he again survived—is proof of von Papen's amazing diplomatic abilities. His tragedy is that he was pitted against Adolf Hitler, a man whose principles and psyche he simply did not understand. It was a situation where he was outgunned and left with damp powder, fighting a battle for which he was clearly unsuited.

When he sat back and looked at his dispositions President Hindenburg was not happy. But he had done the best he could with limited resources and a field of would-be leaders that was growing smaller by the day. He was tired, ready to die, and knew that within a few months it would no longer be his problem.

With Hitler and Frick in key positions in the cabinet and Hermann Göring as Prussian minister of the interior (not a cabinet a post but one that effectively gave him control of the police in most of Germany), Hindenburg and the conservative lobby had delivered Germany into the hands of the Devil. The seeds of dictatorship had been sown.

3. FRIENDS DISUNITED

If Adolf Hitler had ever had a friend then that man would have been Ernst Röhm. Friends of Adolf Hitler were not easy to come by as his personality was such that it kept people at arm's length. That, in itself, was not a problem as nobody really wanted to come too close to the Nazi leader, anyway. Respect him, admire him, hate him or even despise him—fine. But befriend him, no thank you.

Hitler was a loner and did not seem to need others so that between the two views—other people's and his own—what gradually emerged was a self-contained, tightly controlled human being who might ultimately need contact with other people but certainly did not want it. He found all the friendship he required in the music of Wagner and in the admiring glances of the audience when he spoke, either in public or in the privacy of his own home.

In adulthood Hitler had comrades and acquaintances with whom he could debate and argue, something he did incessantly. As an adolescent, he had possessed one or

Ernst Röhm in his tourer.

two minions who would do his bidding and to uplift him whenever he was down or depressed. The common fact about both sets of 'friends' was that Hitler was always in control. But a real friend, someone who would tell him the truth, for good or bad, someone who would support him in times of trouble and yet challenge him if that was what was needed, was a different matter altogether. And the only one ever likely to qualify for that dubious honour was Ernst Röhm.

They were born a few years apart, Hitler in 1889, Röhm two years earlier in 1887. They came one from each side of the Austrian–German border, Hitler born in Braunau am Inn, Röhm in Munich. Their early upbringing was not too different. Both had fathers who were strict disciplinarians and beatings for misdemeanours, real or imagined, were the regular order of the day. Both fathers were minor officials, Hitler's in the customs service, Röhm's in the railway with the result that petty officialdom soured both boys. They had fathers who were unable to leave their status and positions behind them when they closed the doors of their offices and these in-built attitudes from the work base led to rebellion by both Adolf and Ernst.

Neither particularly liked school and they both chose to escape, Hitler by trying for a scholarship at the Academy of Fine Arts in Vienna, Röhm enlisting as a cadet in the Royal Bavarian 10th Infantry Regiment. From that point on, for a while at least, their careers and lives diverged.

Hitler failed to get his scholarship but Röhm was commissioned into the army in March 1908. Hitler lived for a few years as a dropout in doss houses and homeless shelters, living on the money his mother had left him and an irregular income from the sale of hand-painted postcards and drawings.

Röhm spent his formative years in barrack blocks where the concept of 'militarized masculinity' made a great impression on him. It is impossible to say whether or not his homosexuality began in this environment but it is more than likely that it did

When war erupted across Europe both Röhm and Hitler happily went off to fight for Germany. Röhm, already trained, was soon at the front. At Chanot Wood he was badly injured with wounds to the face that left him scarred for life. After treatment he rejoined his unit and in 1916 fought at the murderous battle of Verdun. He was seriously wounded in the chest during the fighting and after recuperating went down with Spanish flu. For a while it looked as if he would die but Röhm was a hard man to kill off. He recovered, was promoted to captain and spent the last part of the war as a staff officer.

Hitler served as a lance-corporal, never rising above that rank as it was felt he did not have the requisite leadership qualities. His comrades found him difficult and hard to relate to so maybe there was an element of truth in that judgement. He spent the war as a runner, a messenger between headquarters and the front line, a role that

A German soldier, killed during the attack on Grevillers, Western Front, 24 August 1918. (Photo Henry Armytage Sanders/ NLNZ)

usually saw him acting alone, without the support of comrades. It was dangerous and often deadly work that regularly left him out in the open, in full view of enemy snipers and riflemen.

In November 1918 he was wounded and gassed, finishing the war blind and in burning pain at a military hospital behind the lines. His physical injuries were temporary enough. Soon the bandages were off and Hitler could see again. Emotionally, however, the damage was irreparable.

Both men won the Iron Cross First Class, something of which they were inordinately proud, and both of them viewed the German defeat as a humiliation and a disaster. After the surrender Röhm became a member of Colonel von Epp's Freikorps while Hitler remained, for a time, in the army. Both were rootless and clearly searching for something to make their lives, suddenly devastated and without direction, more meaningful.

They met for the first time in 1919 as members of the German Workers' Party (the DAP). Hitler, a 'user' of some note, even at this early stage, surprisingly saw a like-spirit in Ernst Röhm. For perhaps the first time in his life he found someone who would not just bow down to him but argue back when the occasion demanded.

Hitler might not have liked it but he admired and respected Röhm for his views and the way that he espoused them.

After Röhm was eventually eliminated, nobody dared to argue with Hitler again or even raise a controversial issue. That was one of the reasons Hitler loved children and got on well with the families of Goebbels and his secretary Martin Borman. Children did not answer back or contradict. Children were safe territory, unlike adults who would betray and let you down according to their own individual needs.

And yet anyone who has ever looked at the lives of Hitler and Röhm surely cannot help feeling that once Röhm had been eliminated the Führer missed his argumentative and opinionated friend. If there is a tragedy in their relationship it has to be that they could not live happily and easily alongside each other.

Both men were dogmatic and opinionated, something that often led to arguments and quarrels. It did not harm their friendship, however, and as that developed both men realized that they had much in common.

Hitler's anti-Semitism grew virulent during these post-war years, probably as a result of the 'stab in the back' myth and the need to blame somebody for Germany's defeat. Prior to the war he had encountered Jews in Vienna, in Munich and other places. He had done business with them, using them as dealers to sell his paintings. During his military service he met and even served under many more. He may not

Hitler loved children: they rarely caused a problem and they certainly did not answer back or contradict him.

Hitler arrives in Munich for a speaking event.

have been particularly fond of the Jewish race but his real hatred only developed in the wake of Germany's defeat.

Röhm was equally as opposed to the Jewish people but, unlike Hitler, he had a clear socialist streak in his personality and while Hitler used violence for his own ends, Röhm loved it. It was a part of him, part of his complex persona. He was, and always remained, a natural street fighter and brawler, the perfect man to take charge of the SA.

After his brief spell of self-imposed Bolivian exile, Röhm returned to Germany in 1931 as chief of staff of the SA. As leader or Führer of the Party, Hitler was technically in charge of the Stormtroopers but everyone knew that the man the SA loved and obeyed was Ernst Röhm.

And so matters stood when Hitler was appointed chancellor in 1933. The street-fighting SA had been a vital component in his rise to power but now the army, the industrialist backers of the Party and President Hindenburg were all clear that Röhm had to go. For his part the chief of staff took the opposite view and wanted nothing more than to absorb the army into his SA, a suggestion that was viewed with horror by traditional members of the officer class. The ground was set for a titanic struggle.

The story of that struggle is told elsewhere in these pages but, whatever else might be said and done, Hitler still valued his friendship with Röhm and if he could help

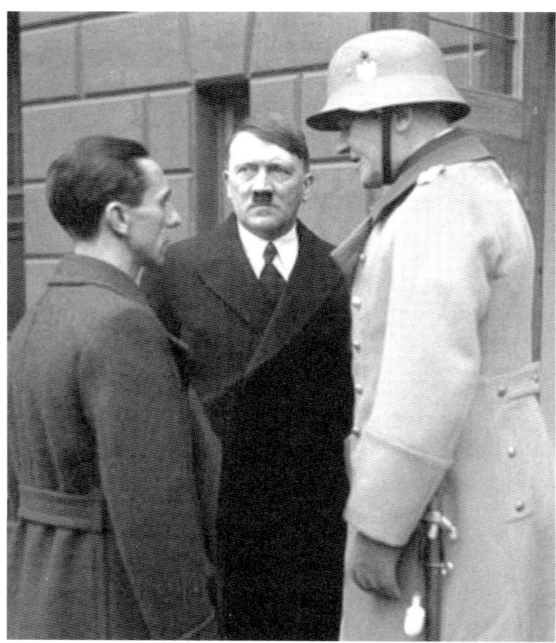

Above left: Hitler at leisure, a Heinrich Hoffman photograph attempting to show the Führer in ordinary pose, just like other ordinary German citizens.

Above right: General von Blomberg towers over Hitler and the Nazi propaganda chief Goebbels.

him find a way out of this potentially damaging situation he would do it. He delayed and prevaricated about dismissing Röhm, almost to the point where his own life and position were in jeopardy.

The pangs and pains of friendship, perhaps the only friendship he had ever known, were haunting Hitler at this time. And it was not easy to bear. He was, almost literally, on the horns of a dilemma. Which way should he go, what should he do?

Whether Röhm felt quite the same is a different matter altogether. There are several recorded instances of Röhm abusing Hitler behind his back, calling him "a shit" and other derogatory terms but by the same token Röhm was the only member of the inner circle ever allowed to use Hitler's first name Adolf or even the nickname Adi. They also addressed each other by the familiar *du*. Hitler, for a while, was genuinely torn between friendship and pragmatism.

By the beginning of 1934 things had reached an impasse, however. Over and above his personal feelings, Röhm was now causing Hitler serious concerns. The chief of staff was becoming increasingly belligerent, making demands—about the army, the status of the SA, his own position—that were impossible to grant.

Hitler found himself being increasingly squeezed between his feelings for Röhm and the pressures and demands of the German state. He tried reasoning with Röhm but it was no use. The SA leader knew what he wanted and nobody, not even Adolf Hitler, was going to stand in his way.

Hitler might demur about the future of the SA but, ultimately, he knew what he would have to do. In February he told Anthony Eden, future prime minister of Britain, that he planned to reduce the SA by two-thirds. Röhm retaliated by further building up the SA's stock of guns and ammunition. Then came the rumour, unacknowledged but probably started by Göring, Himmler or Heydrich, that France had just paid Röhm 12 million marks to mount a coup against the Führer.

Everyone knew, of course, that Röhm was a homosexual. In 1931 the Social Democrat paper *Munchener Post* had actually published private letters they had obtained, sent from Röhm to a friend, discussing homosexual affairs. So it was certainly not a secret; the knowledge was in the public domain. With lordly disdain, Röhm paid the article no heed but the *Munchener Post* had offended Hitler's sensibilities and it was closed down soon after he came to power.

There was nothing unduly feminine about Röhm or his general behaviour and the homosexual act was part of his masculinity, his belief in the warrior code. In many ways it was an extension of the homoeroticism so beloved by the soldier poets of the Great War.

For years now Hitler had turned a blind eye to the issue but, increasingly, he was coming under pressure to do something about the problem of so-called "perversions" in the higher ranks of the Party. It must have seemed, at times, as if everyone was 'ganging up' on him and Röhm, particularly over the matter of sexual deviancy.

Accordingly, regardless of his own feelings on the matter, the regime had already begun to crack down on homosexuals in the months before the Night of the Long Knives. Later, thousands were arrested and it is estimated that between 1939 and 1945 alone as many as 50,000 homosexuals ended up in concentration camps.[*] The situation in 1934 was not nearly so difficult but Röhm must have felt uneasy. Yet he did nothing about it, either in his own personal life or in the behaviour of his senior SA officers.

Sexual deviancy was hardly a major reason for Röhm's fall from grace but his homosexuality undoubtedly played a part. It was, perhaps more than anything, an excuse to act. Ignoring the warning signs, in this as in so many other aspects of his life, was typical of Röhm, a man who on the one hand was able to abuse and denigrate Hitler and on the other declare undying love and affection for him.

---

[*]   daily.jstar.org

A rare photograph of Hitler on a public balcony along with Joseph Goebbels and Ernst Röhm.

When the blow came on 30 June 1934 Röhm could not believe what had happened and was shocked and hurt, probably even traumatized by what his friend Hitler had done to him. It was a degree of naivety that was endemic in his nature and undoubtedly contributed greatly to his ultimate downfall.

Other Nazi leaders, of course, particularly those who had plotted his fall, were far more aware. In 1943, while delivering a speech about the Final Solution to a gathering of Gestapo functionaries, Himmler referred several times to the killings and what he still called the Röhm purge. He was forthright in his beliefs, stating that, "Every single one of us shuddered; nevertheless, each of us understood clearly that he would do it the next time if it were ordered."

The purge, and the subsequent murders that made the Night of the Long Knives such a heinous event, showed quite clearly the levels that the Nazi Party would aim for to protect the State and its own position within it. Hitler might have been troubled, caught like a rabbit in a car's headlights, but in the end he sacrificed friendship for the sake of political ambition and power. It came down, eventually, to what was most important to Hitler: friendship or his standing as the head of the Nazi Party.

After the Night of the Long Knives the amount of State-sponsored terror across Germany rose sharply. The levels of barbarity that the Nazi Party was capable of reaching were clearly mapped out, if anyone had cared to study them. Friendship and ties to the past meant nothing. And neither did the expectations of society. Persecution—of Jews, gypsies, Jehovah Witnesses, homosexuals, retards—became endemic, not because society demanded it but because the Nazi ideology and concept of itself as a world-leading organization would allow nothing less.

The dark nemesis: a portrait of Heinrich Himmler.

The persecution of the Jews and the Holocaust are well documented, with nearly six million innocent Jewish men, women and children victims of the SS Einstazgruppen and the gas chambers of Auschwitz and other death camps. Over 12,000 Jehovah's Witnesses were also imprisoned and thousands died. Even the Catholic Church suffered persecution with the concentration camp at Dachau having a barracks dedicated to imprisoned clergy. By the end of the war it had housed 2,720 clergymen, the vast majority being Catholic. Thousands of gypsies, Romanians and Poles were imprisoned and executed without cause or concern.

Homosexuality had been used as an excuse for the destruction of Röhm and much of the SA but that facade did not hide the homophobic nature of the Nazi regime. In 1938 the number of annual prosecutions of homosexuals reached 8,500 and would have continued to grow had it not been halted by the outbreak of war. As Guido Knopp later wrote: "Himmler ordered that any homosexual who had relations with more than one partner should be sent to concentration camp, without trial. In 1941 homosexual activity between members of the SS was made punishable by death."

Himmler visits Dachau.

It did not matter that many or most of the ideals aimed at by the Nazis were well outside the remit of the law. They were things that had to be done and Röhm, undoubtedly a brutal man, was no different from many later victims of the Nazis. He simply did not realize that he was dealing with men who had little or no compassion, no honour and no basic human decency.

Having made his decision to act, to take out Röhm and the more troublesome members of the SA, even Hitler found that he had to justify his actions—to himself rather than the German people. In his speech to the nation after the purge he was clear why he had acted in the way that he did when other options were actually available: "I was responsible for the German nation and at that moment I was Germany's highest judge."

Despite his own violent nature Röhm had come up against men who would not hesitate to do anything they felt was required to maintain their own position and status. And that included Adolf Hitler. Ernst Röhm, barbaric as he was, probably had more basic humanity.

4. PARAMILITARY MIGHT

Ask anyone to give you their most memorable visual image of Hitler's Germany and the chances are they'll come back with the same one: Leni Riefenstahl's dramatic photographs of Stormtroopers, standing rank upon rigid rank almost as far as the eye can see, at the 1934 Nuremberg Rally. *Triumph of the Will* is an amazing film, one that more than anything gives the viewer the impression of power, raw power bent to one object or desire: worship of the Führer.

The Third Reich was a militaristic society. You can see it in those straight backs and eager faces in Riefenstahl's film. These are men who have sworn loyalty to the Führer and will happily, eagerly, die for him. That loyalty, even though it was initially split between Hitler and Röhm, had been apparent since the early days of the movement.

Faith and loyalty—faith in Hitler's judgement and loyalty to him on a personal level—were the cornerstones of the Nazi movement. Although, within a few years, the army would also swear an oath to the Führer, to begin with it was the paramilitary groups that proclaimed unswerving devotion to their leader. And Hitler exploited it to the full.

The annual Nuremberg Rally was a highlight for all members of the Nazi Party.

The Nazis were not unique in developing paramilitary units. The Freikorps that seemed to proliferate at this time—the brainchild of ex-general Kurt von Schleicher, later chancellor of Germany—were just the tip of a very large iceberg. Free-standing gangs of men who could be put to any task, the Freikorps were right-wing units, violently and bitterly opposed to the communists, with whom they battled on a regular basis. Some Freikorps units, invariably made up of rootless ex-soldiers, were under government control and if so they were paid, usually through army sources. Others were affiliated to organizations like the Nazi Party. These were unpaid, unless the party managed to find funds to reward them, and ran the risk of being banned by the authorities if their activities became too violent.

Hitler's SA fell into this trap and they duly found themselves outlawed at one stage. It was only by the intervention of Franz von Papen who was attempting to curry favour with Hitler that the ban was eventually lifted.

For sheer size, if nothing else, the Sturmabteilung, the SA or Brownshirts as its members were popularly known, was the most important paramilitary organization within Hitler's Germany. Formed in the early days of the Party, the SA grew out of the strong-arm squads led by the ex-convict Emil Maurice. Their purpose, to begin with at least, was to protect Hitler and other Party members but, increasingly, they were used to disrupt the meetings of other political parties and to create a presence on the streets.

Opernplatz, where the Nazis burned over 20,000 books on 10 May 1933. (Photo Jorge Láscar)

Disguised for a time as the Gymnastic and Sports Division of the Party, on 5 October 1921 they formally became the Sturmabteilung. Out in the open now, the SA wore brown uniforms—in a direct 'lift' from Benito Mussolini's Blackshirts in Fascist Italy—and, placed under the command of Johann Ulrich Klintzich, began to contest and, eventually, claim power on the streets.

These men happily carried out Hitler's orders. Only once did he personally lead them in an attack on a rival political group when the speaker, a Bavarian by the name of Otto Ballerstedt, was administered a severe beating and Hitler found himself in prison again. Sentenced to three months, he served just one and emerged from his first experience of 'common jail' more popular than ever. As he told the police, the sentence had been worth it as the SA got what they wanted: Ballerstedt did not speak.

The SA was a loud and violent organization, even more so when Röhm took control. With their brown uniforms and close companionship, their semi-military-style organization and willingness to resort to beatings, brawling and even murder, they were a formidable group. For men who had been rootless and without any sense of purpose ever since their discharge from the military, membership of the SA gave a distinct feeling of belonging.

Persecution of the Jews came quickly in post-Weimar Germany. This shows SA troops blocking and preventing access to Jewish shops.

Members of the SA in front of a Jewish shop during the boycott of Jews in Nazi Germany on 1 April 1933. The sign says: "Germans, Attention! This shop is owned by Jews. Jews damage the German economy and pay their German employees starvation wages. The main owner is the Jew Nathan Schmidt." (Source Yad Vashem)

Unfortunately for Hitler, if there was one man who could claim their affection and loyalty even more surely than the Führer himself, it was Ernst Röhm. This maimed veteran of Verdun scrapped with them on the streets, led them and promised them that, soon, they would receive all that they desired and deserved in life. More than anything he was one of them.

The SA was a vitally important part of the Nazi regime. Without these violent thugs who literally kicked the opposition off the political stage, it is doubtful that the Party would ever have achieved power. However, as a group from within the main organization—a party within a party—they needed careful handling. It was essential that the leadership of the SA was both effective and loyal to Adolf Hitler.

SA violence was always liable to flare up at any moment, something that was acceptable, even necessary, on the long climb to power. Once there, however, when Hitler stood at the peak or the summit of the German political apparatus, the value of the SA was unclear.

The SA was not the only paramilitary organization of note within the Nazi Party. The Schutzstaffel, the SS as they were universally known, were perhaps the most sinister—and certainly the most feared—of all Nazi groups. Dressed in jet-black

A Nazi postcard proclaiming the Nazi message: "One Party, One Fuhrer, One Reich".

uniforms, designed, incidentally, by Hugo Boss, they looked and were terrifying. Formed in 1920 they were, initially, a part of the SA and called the Saal Schutz (Hall Protectors). That was their first role, with a particular mission to support and protect Hitler. They were modelled on the Erhardt Brigade, one of the most infamous Freikorps units of the time, and originally consisted of just eight volunteers. By 1925 the fledgling SS had more than proved its worth; it had now come under the command of the man who was to become infamous and whose name would be forever linked with what grew to be the foremost terror and security agency in the Third Reich: Heinrich Himmler.

Often denigrated by opponents as a "chicken farmer", Himmler, unlike so many other early recruits to the Nazi Party, had not served during the war, being too young to enlist. The chicken farmer allusion was accurate as he had attended agricultural college and set up a poultry farm in the immediate post-war years. He joined the Nazi Party in 1923 and served initially in the SA where his skill in administration and organization were noted.

In 1925 a transfer to the SS, where his devotion to Hitler was instantly obvious, meant promotion and, eventually, elevation to the upper reaches of the Party.

The evil that men do lives after them: the SS.

Infamy and the creation of the death camps came later. For the time being Himmler was happy to serve and support his master.

Made Reichsführer SS in 1929, Himmler was an unprepossessing figure but was not without at least a degree of compassion. Unfortunately that compassion did not often rear its head. He was a man of immense contradictions; a family man who often quailed at the sight of blood, he was also psychotic, murderous and obsessed with making the SS the epitome of Nazi idealism. Members of the SS had to be perfect specimens of Aryan manhood. It was an interesting and contradictory point, given the fact that Himmler himself was undersized and bespectacled.

As far as standard values were concerned, perhaps the most significant characteristic of any SS trooper was his total and unbreakable loyalty to Hitler, one characteristic that Himmler did possess. The blood oath that the SS swore undoubtedly gave the Führer a sense of security, something that he needed badly in the face of Röhm's private army. Under Himmler's careful and meticulous direction, the SS grew in size and strength. Soon it was ready to break away and become a separate organization, independent from the SA. While Röhm was still in control of the Stormtroopers, such independence was not possible. Himmler would have to wait; the time was not quite ripe.

There were three elements to the SS: the general or Allgemeine branch, a military section to rival the army (the Waffen-SS) and, perhaps the deadliest group of all, the Totenkopfverbande (Death's Head) units that ran the concentration camps. The three elements operated on an altogether more intellectual level than the SA, even though the members were as dedicated to Nazism—perhaps more so—as any of their brown-shirted comrades in arms. The SS were Hitler's 'warrior monks' with the organization made up of far more self-controlled and competent individuals than the SA could ever muster.

Members of the SS were selected because of their fanatical support of Nazi ideals and in the relatively short period since its creation, by the end of the 1930s the organization had developed into a cult of terrifying proportions. Much of this status was down to Himmler and, in particular, to his deputy Reinhard Heydrich. Cold, calculating and unswerving in his devotion to Nazi principles, Heydrich was considered by many to be the most evil man in the Reich.

As if the SA and SS were not enough there was a third paramilitary organization that was initially allied to the Nazi Party. This was the Stahlhelm, the Steel Helmets.

Reinhard Heydrich, in the opinion of many the most evil man to hold political office in the Third Reich.

Originally a veterans' group founded after the war and, to begin with, opposed to the Nazis, the Steel Helmets did nevertheless hold similar views to Hitler and his cronies—anti-Semitism and a hatred of communism being just two. Over the years the Steel Helmets grew markedly closer to the Nazis and by 1933 there was little to differentiate between the three paramilitary organizations.

Starting with a membership of under a dozen, the Steel Helmets could eventually call on over 500,000 ex-soldiers to take to the streets whenever occasion demanded it. Membership like that made the Helmets a very desirable ally for Hitler. They were opposed to the liberal democracy of the Weimar Republic which they thought was weak and decadent. They wanted a dictatorship and were prepared to fight for it. They received financial aid from Italy's Benito Mussolini who, for several years, saw the Stahlhelm as more likely to achieve success than Hitler's Nazis.

Although initially a separate entity from the Nazi Party, by the time of Hitler's elevation to power in 1933 the Steel Helmets were happy to lend whatever support was requested by their fellow fascists. Closer and closer links eventually led to them becoming the third paramilitary arm of the Party. In 1934 they were incorporated into the SA and, within a few years, they had no separate entity at all.

The Junkers 52

The famous three-engined Junkers 52 was Hitler's favourite aeroplane. He did not particularly enjoy travelling by train while cars were fine for short journeys but were uncomfortable for anything longer than a few hours. So flying—although he hated to be airborne when it was dark—was his preferred mode of travel.

The Ju 52 was a strange-looking machine, easily identifiable with its one propeller on the fuselage and one on each wing. With seating for 17 passengers the Junkers became synonymous with Hitler's cross-country electioneering during the 1930s, whisking him from one meeting to the next in a matter of two or three hours when travel by car or train would have taken twice as long.

Nicknamed *Tante Ju* ('Aunt Ju'), the Ju 52 was first manufactured in 1931. Originally powered by a single engine, the plane was soon adapted and modified for three, thereby making it safer and faster in the air. It became the primary cargo and troop-carrying aeroplane of the Third Reich and continued in production as a civilian machine after the war ended in 1945.

The Ju 52 was ideal for the dropping of paratroopers. Some were modified into mine-sweeping aircraft, fitted with huge degaussing rings below the fuselage. But it is as Hitler's plane that it will always be remembered. The aircraft had a unique corrugated-iron skin which strengthened the structure of the machine, something that pleased Hitler greatly. For its time it was reasonably fast, able to make the journey from Berlin to Rome in under eight hours. Time was important to Hitler, particularly when he was campaigning all over the country as he did in the 1932 elections. It was also very important during an operation like The Night of the Long Knives.

Hitler's Ju 52, almost always flown by his personal pilot Hans Baur, was named 'Immelmann 11' after Max Immelmann, the original German fighter ace of the Great War. For Hans Baur, himself an air ace from that war, it was the perfect name.

The Fuhrer soon acquired more Junkers aircraft, eventually gathering together approximately fifty of them, all based at Tempelhof airport in Berlin. Other Nazi dignitaries soon followed Hitler's example and the redoubtable Ju 52ss were constantly in the air, taking Göring, Himmler and the rest to meetings all over the country. It was not just the Nazi elite. Luft Hansa, the German airline company, used the Junkers 52 as a luxury airliner and so it was not long before the aircraft was known all over the world. It became popular in countries as far away as China and, just like Hitler before him, the Ju 52 was renowned as the favourite aircraft of Chiang Kai-Shek. In September 1939, just after the outbreak of war, Hans Baur managed to persuade Hitler to replace the Ju 52 with the more modern and safer Focke Wulf Condor. But Hitler remained fond of his Immelmann 11 and kept it as a reserve aircraft until the fall of Berlin in 1945.

The Junkers 52. (Ryan Kirk)

The activities of the three paramilitary groups within the Nazi Party, the SA and SS in particular, inevitably grabbed the headlines and many of Germany's more respectable citizens looked on with amazement as the marching, the beatings and the fighting continued unabated. Was this, they asked themselves, the way politics was supposed to work? And how could someone like Hitler who had promised peace and stability continue to condone such outrages?

As late as 1930 the eye-catching but vicious street battles continued. Over 2,500 members of the Party, most of them SA Stormtroopers, were injured in that single year alone while seventeen were actually killed in street brawls. In June 1932 there were more than 400 such battles across the country, resulting in no fewer than eighty-two deaths across all parties and political groupings.

Röhm, with his decidedly socialist leanings, was always happy to take the side of the workers in any dispute they might have with management or the government. As a consequence, the SA was regularly involved in supporting picket lines and attacking strike-breakers, or scabs.

Small wonder, then, that the capitalists and financiers who were bankrolling the Nazi Party were worried by such actions. Activities like strike-breaking and destroying opposition groups were against all their interests. If that had been all, fine, but there was also the lack of control and the sheer hooliganism of the paramilitary units. Increasingly, as Röhm's belligerence grew, the behaviour of the SA began to cause the financiers great concern. And it was not just physical violence against political opposition or the small Jewish enclaves that worried them. Structural violence, an automatic and insistent violence perpetrated by the system or by the State, became endemic in Germany in the 1930s after Hitler came to power. It manifested itself in the attitudes of Party members where one view—and one view alone—was expected and tolerated. It was not restricted to the physical beating of opponents but was rather more subtle in its application. Not a member of the Nazi Party? Don't look for promotion here. You have Jewish origins? You're out of a job. Forget what you learned before, this is the curriculum you will now study in school or university. And as far as jazz and other examples of degenerate 'Negro music' are concerned, don't even think of it. There's no place for that in the new Germany. And so on.

One of the more obvious signs of structural, or institutionalized, violence came in the way that literature was dealt with and regarded. An orchestrated programme of book burning began in 1933, soon after Hitler became chancellor. It saw the SA, supported by groups of right-wing students, consign any undesirable writings, Jewish writings in particular, to the bonfires that sprang up in many of the university cities across the country. It was barbarism, a total lack of empathy toward

Book burning on the streets of Germany, circa 1934.

culture, and was something which many intellectuals, industrialists and capitalists viewed with horror. There were no words to describe their feelings as the works of writers like Martin Luther, Thomas Mann and Sigmund Freud were consigned to the flames. It was not as if the industrialists were great lovers of literature or culture, although most of them probably owned collections of rare books and paintings. The book burning was, however, the tip of the iceberg: books today, what comes tomorrow?

Hitler knew that it would not take much for the industrialists, the great owners and employers from the steel mills and production centres throughout Germany, to withdraw their support. There was a delicate line to be walked if he was to keep the backers on his side as the whole future of the Party depended on regular contributions from these men.

These backers were not philanthropists. They were right-wing businessmen who were, obviously, keen to make money. In order to do that they needed to see industrial plants revived and German steel and coal sold abroad. That meant creating the right ambience in the workforce and making a solid commitment to rebuild German industry. The Nazis seemed to be the most likely bet to create such an environment but they were not the only option. The businessmen were wary. Nobody was going to buy from a disorganized rabble, people like Krupp, Messerschmitt and Farben told Hitler, or make investments where the rule of gun and bullet had succeeded the rule of the law; we will give you money and our backing, they promised, but you have to do something about the behaviour of the Brownshirts.

They were not talking small donations to the Party, either, these factory owners and capitalists, these power houses from the world of big business. In 1933 the Ruhr Combine alone promised a million marks to the Party funds while IG Farben unconditionally gifted half a million. Hitler could not afford to sniff at sums of money like that. But when some hothead like Ernst Röhm began talking of a second revolution or the need to nationalize businesses, Krupp, Farben and the others were immediately on their guard. They were not so short-sighted or masochistic as to even think of paying out vast sums of cash simply to help in their own demise.

Ernst Röhm, shortly before his murder.

Despite their automatic preference for the Nazi Party the men of the capitalist Right did have concerns that went beyond the rowdy behaviour of the Stormtroopers. For a long while there was a general fear of a communist fifth column existing inside the Nazi Party and it was a concern that was not without some foundation, particularly as far as the SA was concerned.

Unlike the predominantly middle-class SS, the Brownshirts had a basically working-class background and membership. As might be expected, hundreds of its members had actually been communists in the past and there was even a rumour that Hitler himself had once been a member of a communist group. There was no easy answer to the problem, a situation that gave rise to the jibe that many members of the SA were "beefsteak Nazis—brown on the outside, red inside." Such men and their beliefs, latent or otherwise, were abhorrent to the wealthy industrialists. And the constant flow of socialist jargon from Röhm was certainly not calculated to keep matters calm. No amount of cajoling or persuasion from his friend Hitler could prevent Röhm from making his point, both in public speeches and in private.

It was not just the industrialist backers of the Party who were worried. Under the terms of Article 160 of the Treaty of Versailles, Germany's regular army had been reduced to just 100,000 men and by the early 1930s they were vastly outnumbered by the SA which was now gleefully rejoicing at a figure of over three million Stormtroopers in its ranks. Röhm had been assiduously arming his men for many months, passing on guns and weaponry from the Bavarian armoury—with which he still had contacts. It was an illegal process but Röhm was never going to quibble at that and even as Hitler was taking the last steps to power he continued to arm his SA units. Not for nothing was he known as "The machine gun King of Bavaria."

The SA was supposed to be armed with nothing more dangerous than knuckle dusters and clubs—in fact it was equipped with rifles, heavy machine guns, hand grenades and other lethal armaments, all thanks to Ernst Röhm. By 1934 it had become the SA leader's private army. They might have been well armed but the SA brawlers could not hope to compete with the army in terms of artillery or support weapons—or for that matter in military tactics.

Despite being severely handicapped by a crippling lack of heavy weapons, the Treaty of Versailles had allowed the Reichswehr to train and carry out military manoeuvres, but much to the chagrin of the German high command the terms of the Treaty of Versailles stipulated no tanks and no heavy artillery. Only a few light field guns, several infantry battalions and the much-loved cavalry units—from which most of the senior Reichswehr officers came—were all they could gather together in the event of trouble. Even so they would still have been more than a match for Röhm's street brawlers and rabble rousers. In fact, the only real advantage that the SA had over the army lay simply in their superiority of numbers. And that was significant.

The officer class of the Reichswehr was unashamedly conservative. The lives of officers, from generals down to subalterns, were lived around the reassuring totems of tradition and aristocratic behaviour so the beer-swilling Stormtroopers of the SA were hardly likely to endear themselves to such men. The SA was, to the officers of the Reichswehr, simply a barbaric and self-interested group of street ruffians. To some extent the opinion was accurate. The street fighting battlers of the SA were undoubtedly little more than bands of thugs, albeit organized and powerful thugs with clear leadership and lines of communication.

It remains strange to think that the SA did actually pose a threat to the army. It was not just idle rhetoric and Röhm, in particular, was vocal in his demands to subsume the Reichswehr into the ranks of his Stormtroopers—not the other way around. It was hardly surprising when his Brownshirts outnumbered the regular army by at least ten to one. The idea of being taken over by the Stormtroopers terrified the senior army officers.

The concept of a socialist–nationalist military force was no passing fancy and it soon became a notion that lodged itself at the forefront of Röhm's mind. He had served in the trenches with the regular army and had been wounded at Verdun. He had seen the supercilious officer corps at work—and he did not like it. Ernst Röhm, with clear visions of his own position in the Reich, was not the type of man to let go of such an idea.

After Hitler's assumption of power, the idea of an SA takeover did not diminish, it actually grew stronger. Just prior to The Night of the Long Knives in June 1934 the fear reached its height, as General Edward von Kleist later wrote: "Round about 24 June, as the army commander in Silesia, I was warned by the Chief of the General Staff [Ludwig Beck] that an attack by the SA on the German army was imminent and that I should unobtrusively keep my troops on the alert. During the tense days that followed I received a flood of reports and information which gave a picture of feverish preparations on the part of the SA."

The original document, outlining the SA's intentions, had been unearthed by the Abwehr, the army intelligence unit which had dubious credentials and was markedly inefficient right to the end of the Third Reich. Its ineptitude was hardly surprising when Abwehr commander Admiral Canaris was violently opposed to Hitler and the Nazis and may even have doubled as a British spy. It was quite possible that nobody in the Abwehr actually knew where the document came from. Whatever its origins, dubious or genuine, the Abwehr duly passed it on to Beck.

Nothing came of von Kleist's concerns and the activity he wrote about might well have been early preparation for the Night of the Long Knives. It might have been sheer panic or it might have been the result of clandestine action by Röhm's colleagues within the Nazi Party. It is almost certain that the rumours, and the document, originated from SS leaders Heinrich Himmler and Reinhard Heydrich, a scheming and devious pair of miscreants, now sitting contentedly at the top of the SS. They were a deadly duo, as time was to prove, who regularly went as far as to brief senior army officers about Röhm's intentions. Their motives were not designed for the good of Germany or the army and the documentation and the rumours were undoubtedly spurious, sheer fabrications from the SS. The fact that the army believed them probably says more about military anxieties than it does about the viability of the lies.

Despite his pronouncements and despite arming his SA Stormtroopers, it was highly unlikely that Röhm had any plans to mount a coup. From the time such a move was first rumoured until the moment of his death the SA leader strenuously denied any intention of undermining the Führer. He was, he declared, loyal to the Party, to Hitler and to Germany.

Over and over again Ernst Röhm stressed that loyalty. It hardly mattered. In the tense and fragile atmosphere of Germany in the early days of Hitler's chancellorship it was fear that was the most significant factor, not the reality.

He might have been loyal—and the evidence all seems to point to the fact that he was, indeed, a loyal supporter and friend of the Führer—but there was no doubt that Röhm had seriously underestimated his opponents, both within and outside the Party. In 1934, as winter turned to spring, slowly but surely the levels of fear and suspicion mounted.

Heinrich Himmler and others close to Hitler had spent months happily stoking that fear. As early as January 1934 their whispers had begun to have an effect. In the words of Ian Kershaw: "According to the later account of Gestapo chief Rudolf Diels, it was in January 1934 that Hitler requested him and Göring to collect material on the excesses of the SA. From the end of February onwards the Reichswehr leadership started assembling its own intelligence on SA activities, which was passed to Hitler."

The Gestapo had been founded by Göring in 1933 as the political or state police department in Prussia. Like so many other aspects of Göring's life and career, the mercurial former air

A portrait photograph of the arch-manipulator Herman Göring.

ace could never maintain an interest or a passion for long and already he was becoming bored with his new creation. Himmler, looking to extend and develop his SS organization, was beginning to take over control of every police force in the Reich and Göring saw an opportunity.

He was more than happy to barter the Prussian Gestapo and allow the bespectacled "chicken farmer" to become inspector general of the force. This made Himmler effectively second in command of the Gestapo, behind the disinterested and increasingly more and more distanced Göring himself. In exchange Göring expected Himmler's support in getting rid of Ernst Röhm. To Himmler, Göring and the like it was all grist to their political and personal mills. They revelled in the mire of plot and counterplot and the more apprehension, the more terror that they could create then the less objective people's judgement was going to be when it came to making crucial policy and practical decisions.

Himmler, of course, had his own agenda and was cleverly playing both sides against the middle. He had no desire to slip back into the anonymity of the SA. He had nailed his colours to the mast and had no qualms in admitting that his future lay with the SS. He was already heavily engaged in the process of building a nation-wide force of secret service men, police and enforcers that would ensure his safety and his position within the Reich. It can be argued that he, far more than Hitler, was the true manifestation of evil in the State. Himmler's real love, however, was the SS. Often he personally selected new members and was at his happiest when he was in the company of his hand-picked entourage.

As a terror organization and as the apogee of Aryan manhood, even at this early stage the SS was being seen as a force apart, a higher echelon in German society. A veneer of power and untouchable prestige settled early on the members of the SS; and that was something nobody, from Hitler and Himmler down to the newest recruit, was ever going to challenge. Himmler had begun to plant and cultivate the totally fabricated but happily accepted mythology of the organization, its origins and its birth right, within the consciousness of SS members and the German people in general. Secret rituals, the startling Hugo Boss uniforms, even the fabricated spiritual home of the organization in a Black Forest castle, they all contributed to making the SS a force apart.

Like Göring—who did genuinely fear for his life at the hands of Röhm—Himmler was a master intriguer and his game was cunningly played. He knew that the greatest threat to his progress within the Nazi Party was always going to be the SA. Therefore they and Ernst Röhm in particular, needed to be neutralized as quickly as possible, neutralized in a way that would allow not even the faintest hint of a comeback. Strange as it might seem, the biggest stumbling block to Himmler's plans was actually Adolf Hitler. Himmler's loyalty to the Führer was not in doubt; as far as he was concerned the future of the Party and of Germany lay in Hitler's hands. But Himmler knew his man and was clear that Hitler needed incontrovertible proof before he would even think of acting against Röhm. Convincing Hitler to take any action that did not come from his own fertile but twisted brain was difficult. It was not something that could be done in a matter of minutes. Hitler needed time to digest information, to sit and consider and to formulate his views. In the meantime it was best to keep Röhm happy.

Only a few days before General von Kleist was warned about SA preparations, Himmler and Karl Wolff, one of his SS subordinates, had visited Röhm and begged him to disassociate himself from the more disreputable elements of the SA. Although they came under the guise of old Party comrades, their purpose was anything but friendly. Excessive use of alcohol, vandalism and dalliance in such sexual perversions as homosexuality, Himmler and Wolff declared, were bringing the whole movement into disrepute. There was still time to curb the excesses of the SA—and, of course, his own personal predilections—but Röhm would have to act now if he was going to retain Hitler's affection and trust.

Röhm's sexual preferences had been common knowledge for years. As long as the SA chief was useful, Hitler had chosen to ignore these foibles but things had moved on. Different times needed a different approach and it was now time to use these perversions, as the Party labelled them, as a stick to batter Röhm and all of his colleagues in the SA.

Do not give me the burden of having to go my people, the SS, Himmler charitably stated. Do not force me to get them to act against you. Old comrades did not deserve that.

Röhm thanked Himmler for the warning and the three men parted with tears—crocodile tears undoubtedly—in their eyes. Röhm promptly forgot or shelved the warning and Himmler and Wolff went away rubbing their hands, feeling that they had pulled the wool over the eyes of the SA leader.

With both sides, the army and the SA, now on high alert, the time had finally come for Hitler to act. Göring, Himmler and Heydrich had done their work and done it effectively. Hitler had endured Röhm and his rabble rousers for long enough. Röhm had seriously damaged the standing and the position of the Party. He had ignored Hitler's requests for moderation and was unable to see that while his longed-for second revolution would eventually occur it would be a gradual process rather than a violent uprising. As it happened, the demise of Ernst Röhm was one of the seminal moments in that second revolution. And that was something not even he could have foreseen.

Adverts from the Sturm Cigarette Co., the Sturmabteilung's own cigarette manufacturer, which provided most of their operating funds. This ad is from December 1933, after the Nazis took power. It shows new cigarette packs, holding six cigarettes apiece, and prices in pfennigs per cigarette. Pack and cigarette carry the SA logo. The slogan reads *"Wer sie einmal wählt, ist ihr immer verbunden"*, which might be translated as "Choose them once, be bound to them forever". It could also be translated as "Vote for them once, be obliged to them forever". The word *verbunden* carries connotations of social connection and fraternity; a *verband* is a formal alliance or organization, such as the SA.

5. MURDER AND MAYHEM AT BAD WIESEE

As it turned out it was the army that finally forced Hitler's hand but, even then, he made his decision only after much head scratching. Despite how history later labelled him, Adolf Hitler was by nature an indolent and indecisive character. He did not like making the decision but when all the prevarication, the interminable discussions and soul searching were said and done, the Führer was left with no choice other than to act against the SA. Quite when the decision was made to cull Röhm and his compatriots remains unknown but it was certainly late in the countdown to destruction. Arguably it was on the night of 28 June that Hitler finally nodded his approval.

In early June 1934 Vice-Chancellor Franz von Papen had managed to summon up enough courage to challenge Hitler in a speech given at Marburg University. In that

speech von Papen was scathing and condemnatory of the Nazi leader's inability to take criticism. He also decried the negative course of the so-called "German revolution" and the unscrupulous and disgraceful behaviour of the SA. Hitler and leading members of the Party were furious.

Goebbels immediately banned publication of the speech. Von Papen and Edgar Jung, co-author of the missive, suddenly realized that they were on a very slippery slope. Von Papen, Hitler declared, was a pygmy but when the vice-chancellor visited the Chancellery to express his concern about the repression of his speech and offer his resignation the Führer played him like a puppy. He was placatory and promised to lift the ban on the speech –after all, this was a democracy, wasn't it? Ever conscious

Edgar Jung, critic of the Nazi Party, was shot during the purge.

of what President Hindenburg might say, he also persuaded von Papen to delay his resignation, at least for a little while.

Edgar Jung did not even warrant a comment. If Papen was a pygmy, Jung was an even lower life form but, even so, he was marked down for "treatment" when the time was ripe.

Von Papen had been doing no more than expressing the concerns of the German people as a whole. More important to Hitler, however, was the opinion of the president, the aged and ailing Field Marshal Paul von Hindenburg. Hitler had heard rumours that Hindenburg was displeased with what was a seemingly never-ending tide of violence and with the way the country was being governed. It would take only the wrong word at the wrong time and he would be dismissed, like von Schleicher before him, ruining years of slow and painful preparation for power.

Alarmed at the danger, on 21 June Hitler flew to Neudeck to discuss the situation with the president. He was met by General von Blomberg of the Reichswehr who briefly and succinctly told him exactly what he did not want to hear. Von Blomberg informed Hitler that "unless the present state of tension in Germany was brought quickly to an end, the president would declare martial law and turn over control of the state to the army".

General von Blomberg, chief of the German military until a scandal in his personal life— his wife, the Nazis discovered, had once been a prostitute—forced his resignation.

When Hitler was finally ushered into Hindenburg's presence, the old man simply confirmed von Blomberg's statement. An army-run state was the last thing Hitler wanted and he came away much chastised, determined, as soon as he was able, to destroy the position of Reich president. That was a longer-term aim. For the moment he had much more immediate matters to contend with.

Hitler had already debated the idea of disposing of the office of president. In April he had spent six days on the pocket battleship *Deutschland* along with Admiral Raeder and generals von Fritsch and von Blomberg, supposedly watching spring manoeuvres in East Prussia but in reality negotiating the amalgamation of the two top posts in Germany, the chancellorship and the presidency—with himself as the holder of the new position.

In exchange for the agreement of the military Hitler had proposed a huge expansion of the army and navy, a subject dear to the hearts of all the military men who were present. He had even tentatively discussed the idea of curbing the power of the SA. Now that really caught the attention of the army. His plans were, therefore, already forming. The very last thing Hitler needed now was for Röhm and his Stormtroopers to cause too many ripples.

Back in Berlin, he immediately went into a meeting with Göring and Himmler. Like Hitler they were amazed at Hindenburg's words but they were also delighted. This was the opportunity for which they had been waiting for several months. Without formality and barely able to hide their glee, they inundated the Führer with dozens of forged letters and documents implicating

Hitler on the telephone. A rare photograph— he is smiling.

Röhm as the leader of a proposed coup against Hitler and the Party. Their forgers had done a magnificent job. All of the dates fitted and even Röhm's signature appeared to be totally genuine.

As the sky over Berlin turned grey, then blue as dawn finally punched its customary holes into the canvas of the night, Hitler's lack of resolve and indecisiveness gradually vanished. He was sure now that Röhm and the SA had betrayed him and placed his position as chancellor in jeopardy. He had tried to protect them and even at this late stage, for a brief moment at least, he felt that removing Röhm from the leadership of the SA might be enough. Over the next few days he was disabused of that idea by Göring and Himmler.

A secret meeting was immediately arranged with leaders of the army. The military would support him, Hitler was told, but there was a condition: he would have to rid the government and Germany of that continuing curse, the SA. Still furious at Röhm's supposed betrayal, Hitler agreed. In many respects it was still a bitter pill for Hitler to swallow. He and the SA had grown together from political novices to men of power and position. The journey had been mutually beneficial. And in all fairness the communists were as much to blame as the SA for the violence and disorder on Germany's streets.

In the days after Hitler came to power communists been planning a programme of demonstrations, public meetings and rallies. Some groups were even intending to begin outbreaks of arson. Their proposed actions had been monitored by the Gestapo but the communist campaign and opposition to Hitler's elevation to the top post was only halted by the Reichstag fire.

The fire was, depending on your stance, either a miraculous piece of good fortune for the Nazis or a brilliantly contrived and beautifully timed piece of covert action. On the evening of 27 February 1934 a Dutchman by the name of Marinus van der Lubbe had stolen into the empty Reichstag building and, using his shirt and four packets of fire-lighters, managed to start a fire that was soon out of control. With the building left as a mass of rubble and iron, Hitler seized the moment to declare a state of emergency.

The Reichstag fire.

The Reichstag Fire Decree and the Enabling Law, legally passed by the members of the Reichstag as they sat in the their temporary parliament building, the nearby Kroll Opera House, gave total and supreme power to Hitler, superseding the constitution of the Weimar Republic. The fact that Göring and the Berlin section of the SA were probably behind van der Lubbe's arson attack was conveniently ignored and the authority to carry out pogroms like the Night of the Long Knives had been firmly placed in Hitler's hands.

From that moment on, until the end of the Nazi Party in 1945, Hitler ruled Germany by decree. The Reichstag committed political suicide when, shortly afterward, they voted to dissolve themselves: it was the final stage in the destruction of German democracy.

*

Throughout the hot spring and summer of 1934 the relationship between Hitler and Röhm remained uneasy. The SA leader had continued with his demands to place the army under his control. Hitler had refused, the two men quarrelled and on 7 June Röhm announced that he was taking sick leave.

Arguments between Hitler and Röhm were not unusual, neither was the SA leader's next move, to flounce away in a sulk. He had done that before, in 1925, and ended up in Bolivia. What was unusual now was his decision about the SA. The Stormtroopers,

Röhm and von Spitz, one of his aides.

81

he said, would also be stood down, taking a well-earned break before returning to duty at the beginning of August. The SA, he declared as a parting shot, would always be Germany's destiny.

Perhaps, in many ways, Röhm was right. The SA did need a break; they had been bullying and battling away for some time now. Yet the timing was bizarre. To stand down your own private army at the moment of deepest crisis smacked either of over-confidence or a degree of fatalism almost akin to a death wish. Hitler, for one, could not understand it but he was willing to go along with his long-time colleague.

The atmosphere in government circles had been strained and to begin with Hitler undoubtedly felt that a little distance would do both parties the world of good, at least until August. Then the machinations of Himmler and Göring began to bear fruit, the army delivered its ultimatum and it became clear that for Röhm and many SA leaders there would be no August.

On 28 June Röhm was expelled from the German Officers' League. A day later an article by General von Blomberg in the *Volkischer Beobachter* made the situation totally clear. The army stood firmly behind Adolf Hitler. He was, von Blomberg wrote, "one of ours", an unusual epithet to award a former corporal when Ernst Röhm had also been a military man but one of considerably higher rank.

Both incidents should have alerted Röhm to the danger. Unfortunately the ruthless and hot-headed Röhm had never been good at picking up signals or hints and, after all, it was barely six months since the Führer had appointed him as minister without portfolio to his cabinet. He had always been supremely confident in his own ability and did not, for one second, believe that Hitler and the Nazi Party would be able to survive without him. Instead of taking decisive action to prevent disaster, Röhm decided that he would relax at the town of Bad Wiesee on the shores of Lake Tegernsee. There he would take the waters in this famous little spa community just a few miles outside Munich and stay in comfort at his favourite lodging, the Hanselbauer Hotel.

It was an idyllic setting. The town was small and private, with discreet staff in its shops, beer gardens and hotels. For those who wanted them, there were long and isolated walks among the giant fir trees that had always been so spiritually symbolic for the Nazis. Forests and shaded groves with their mythological associations immediately brought Wagnerian dreams and ideals to the minds of most right-wing Nationalists. Hitler in particular had always been fascinated by such scenery. It was a pretty area, the traditional and beautifully decorated houses of Bad Wiesee lying clustered along the lake with the foothills of the northern Alps in the background. The hills and slopes were painted by firs and by forests of deciduous trees which, that June, were already in full leaf. The place was redolent of Bavaria and German culture, painting a picture as pure and wholesome as to be almost a cliché.

Röhm was relaxing in this south German paradise when he was contacted by Hitler. He wanted, the Führer declared, to sort out the bad feelings that had grown up in the past few months and, despite the fact that Röhm was on sick leave, he proposed a meeting. So as not to put him out, the meeting could take place at Röhm's hotel and if the chief of staff would contact his senior officers and ask them to attend the summit Hitler would be most grateful.

Röhm readily agreed and as soon as he put down the telephone began issuing orders for all the senior SA officers in Bavaria to come to Bad Wiesee. The message was clear: drop what you are doing, get to the Hotel Hanselbauer where important things are about to happen.

The meeting was set for the following afternoon, the 30th of June, and Röhm went to bed happy and convinced that he had gained the upper hand. After all, Adolf had not summoned him to Munich or Berlin. He had agreed to come to Bad Wiesee and that, Röhm thought, had to be a good sign.

*

It was 6.30 in the morning on the last day in June when Hitler smashed open Röhm's bedroom door at the Hotel Hanselbauer. There was venom in his eyes and hate in his words: "You are a traitor, Röhm, and are under arrest." The SA leader, still half asleep, responded to the interruption with the mumbled standard greeting of "Heil, mein Führer."

At the same time SS troops and plain clothes Gestapo officers were rudely awakening the rest of the SA leaders who had taken rooms in the hotel. It was all over in minutes, doors smashed open, sleeping men dragged from their beds with virtually no protests and little sign of anyone resisting arrest. It was as if nobody could quite believe what was happening.

A bus was rented from a local contractor. Battered and badly painted, it was hardly the height of luxury but by this stage nobody, neither the captives nor their SS captors, cared very much about that and within the hour all the SA prisoners and their guards were en route for gaol in Munich.

So confident had Röhm been in his own invincibility that he had left his personal bodyguards behind in Munich when he decamped to the Hotel Hanselbauer to take the waters. Sitting in the bus on that bright June morning with SS machine guns pointed at his back he must have bitterly regretted that decision. Even so, as they now sped back to the city, salvation almost fell into Röhm's lap.

The convoy of captured SA officers in their bus, flanked and led by Hitler's SS and Gestapo in their traditional black Mercedes tourers, had not gone far when they came

Herman Göring's car, shown here after it had been appropriated by the U.S. military in 1945 and put to use.

nose to nose with a truck carrying Röhm's neglected guards. The arrests in Munich had begun early that morning and the bodyguards had become aware that something serious was happening. They were on their way to Bad Wiesee to rescue or at least help their chief but, as William L. Shirer wrote: "The presence of Hitler appears to have overawed them, for they meekly returned to the city when ordered to do so by the Führer, even though they likely had enough firepower to wipe out Hitler and his small platoon of SS."

Once in Munich Röhm and his men were taken to Stadelheim prison and left to contemplate their fate. Meanwhile, all over the city and throughout Bavaria arrests continued. Swiftly and efficiently, the SS and Gestapo struck, at railway stations, in offices, on the street and in the homes of the unsuspecting victims. By the end of the day over 200 SA leaders had been locked away behind the grim walls of Stadelheim and other prisons.

There was never any intention of putting the captives in front of a court and no advocates ever tested the weight of evidence against them. None of the prisoners was allowed the dignity of being questioned and given the right to speak, in open court, in their own defence. From the moment of their arrest they were condemned men.

The Enabling Laws had given Hitler the power and authority to take such high-handed action in the defence of the nation and over the first forty-eight hours of the operation most of the men arrested were eliminated. It was quick and it was efficiently done. According to the decrees that had given Hitler ultimate power it was almost legal. It was also terribly bloodthirsty and brutal.

Surprisingly, Ernst Röhm was not one of the first to die. Hitler, presumably with some thought of their long-standing companionship and memories of Röhm's previous service to the Party, did not have the heart to order his execution—at least not yet. Others were not so lucky.

After his encounter with the SA bodyguard on the road from Bad Wiesee Hitler returned to the Brown House, the Nazi Party HQ in Munich. At midday he spoke to SA leaders and Party officials, denouncing the so-called "Röhm Plot" and, in a fury of anger, promised retribution. All of the conspirators, he screamed, would be shot. The ever-faithful Rudolph Hess and Max Amann even offered to shoot Röhm themselves. Whether Hitler was really beside himself with fury remains an imponderable. He was an actor of some skill and the situation demanded, at least, a show of righteous anger. Even now Hitler did not take Hess and Amann up on their offer and at no time did he indicate his agreement with Röhm's death, which might give some indication that he was still in control of his emotions.

Instead of Röhm, six SA men out of those currently being held in Stadelheim Prison were marked down for execution, Hitler himself putting crosses on a list that contained their names. The six men were taken outside, told they had been condemned to death by the Führer and shot.

Dozens of others followed the first six. Obergruppenführer Schneidhuber, the man who had first incurred Hitler's wrath earlier that morning, died not knowing what he had done or why he was being executed by men he had believed to be comrades. His final words were, "Gentlemen, I don't know what this is all about, but shoot straight."

With the purge well and truly begun and the most dangerous members of the SA already in custody, Hitler did manage to make it back to Oberwisen airfield by late afternoon on 30 June, exactly as he had intended. Baur, his pilot, had spent the intervening hours, as Hitler had suggested, at home in Munich and knew almost nothing about the purge until he returned to the aircraft at 4 p.m. He was told scraps as he sat in the Junkers, making preparations for takeoff.

It was 10 p.m. before Hitler was back in his capital. Baur had been waiting all day, twiddling his thumbs, and then had to risk a night flight with his chief. Hitler, always nervous of flying in the dark, spent most of the flight prowling around the aircraft cabin or sitting anxiously in his seat. But they made it. Tired, unshaven, the adrenalin beginning to ease from his body, Hitler was met at the airfield by a guard of honour and by Göring and Himmler.

A group photograph showing, among others, von Blomberg and Goebbels.

And now the pressure to dispatch Ernst Röhm really came on. Even so, it was not until the afternoon of the following day, 1 July, during a formal garden party for members of the cabinet and their families that Hitler finally decided that Röhm must die. Even then there were conditions. Whether it was out of decency or from a misguided sense of honour is not clear but Hitler insisted that his old comrade should be left with at least a shred of dignity and pride. *Time* magazine reported: "The Chancellor tried his hardest to make Colonel [sic] Röhm shoot himself, twice sent him a pistol which came back with the reply 'If I am to be shot Hitler will have to do it himself.'"

The story seems genuine enough. Theodor Eicke, the commandant of Dachau concentration camp outside Munich, was the man charged with taking the gun and the message to Röhm. Accompanied by his deputy Michael Lippert, Eike entered Röhm's cell and told him what Hitler wanted. He then left the cell, leaving behind a pistol containing one round and the latest edition of *Volkischer Beobachter* which gave the details of the attempted putsch. It is doubtful that Röhm even opened the paper; he certainly did not touch the gun.

After waiting ten minutes and hearing no shot, Eike and Lippert returned to the cell. Both of them was now carrying drawn and loaded pistols. Röhm rose from the bed where he had been sitting and faced them. His shirt was wide open and he stood defiantly with his chest puffed out. At this last moment of his life, he attempted to say something. It was unlikely to have been an apology or plea for mercy but he never got the chance to speak. Eike had had enough. Both men fired into Röhm's exposed chest and the SA leader fell dead on the cell floor.

Ernst Röhm was many things—violent, arrogant, unimaginative, and possibly even a little stupid. But he was also brave. The moment he was incarcerated in Stadelheim prison he must have known his likely fate. He could have thrown himself on Hitler's mercy but he did not. He stood at attention as Eike and Lippert pointed their guns and reportedly gasped "Mein Führer" as he died. With him went the last possible opposition to Hitler's rule.

Not that Röhm would have been much different as a leader. If anything he was more violent and driven than his old comrade and the death camps and the purges against Jews and other minority groups would probably still have happened. Regardless of that, Röhm was the only Nazi with a following strong enough to challenge Hitler. He was

Theodore Eike, commandant of Dachau concentration camp and undoubtedly the perpetrator of many murders during the Night of the Long Knives.

also the only one with a big enough personality to appeal to the German people. Whether or not he would have actually rebelled against his friend is a totally different matter.

Did Röhm plan a putsch against Hitler? Maybe yes, maybe no; however you look at it, the answer has to be a definite maybe. Despite his protestations of loyalty, right to the end he remained something of an idealist. In January 1934, just a few months before his own murder, he spoke to Kurt Ludecke, a Nazi supporter who was to later write about the conversation, and made his position totally clear: "Hitler can't walk over me as he might have done a year ago; I've seen to that. Don't forget that I have three million men ... If Hitler is reasonable I shall settle the matter quietly; if he isn't I must be prepared to use force."

That could have been typical Röhm bluster. It could just as easily have been a real intention to use force to gain what he wanted; after all, the use of violence came as naturally to Ernst Röhm as breathing.

Perhaps the most telling fact is that Hitler and the Party never produced any actual evidence of Röhm's intentions. There can be little doubt that if any had existed the Führer would certainly have used it to further cement his position. Putsch or no putsch, Hitler's real motive behind destroying Röhm and downgrading the SA was to placate the senior officers in the Reichswehr and to keep Hindenburg off his back. Ernst Röhm, to use jargon that he would certainly have understood, was to be the 'patsy', no more, no less. Whatever his intentions, Röhm was now dead. And Hitler, while regretting that fact was realistic enough to know that, for the Nazi Party and for his own position as leader, the execution had been for the best. There were things that Hitler was to lament in his life but killing Röhm was not one of them.

Reinhard Heydrich: The Man with the Iron Heart

Reinhard Heydrich, Himmler's deputy and architect of the Holocaust, was probably the darkest of all the dark figures of the Third Reich, Hitler himself declaring that he was "the Man with the Iron Heart". Like Heinrich Himmler he played a vital but devious part in the Night of the Long Knives and was instrumental in the destruction of Ernst Röhm. His rewards were significant. Unlike the unfortunate Röhm, Heydrich went on from one piece of evil to another. For a long while nothing seemed able or likely to touch him. Above all, Reinhard Heydrich was the man who chaired the Wannsee Conference in the early days of the Second World War. It was a seminal meeting, the conference being where the fate of the Jewish people and the finer details of the 'Final Solution' were ironed out. Adolf Eichmann and other high-powered Nazi bureaucrats were present at the meeting but there is no doubt about who was pulling the strings and directing proceedings.

In 1932 Himmler had made Heydrich chief of the Reich Main Security Office (*Reichssicherheitshauptamt* or RSHA) which included the dreaded Gestapo. Over the next few years it was Heydrich who developed the infamous Security Service (*Sicherheitsdienst* or SD), making him the most feared man in Germany as the SD grew into a machine of terror and intimidation.

Reinhard Heydrich was born in 1904 and was too young to fight in the Great War but in 1922 he joined the German navy. He rose quickly and by 1928 had achieved the rank of sub-lieutenant. Unfortunately for him he was an arrogant womanizer who then became involved with the Nazi sympathizer Lina von Osten. When Heydrich and Lina announced their engagement his superiors decided it was time to take a hand. The announcement of Heydrich's engagement effectively broke his promise of marriage to another woman and Admiral Raeder had no hesitation in dismissing him from the navy for conduct unbecoming of an officer and gentleman.

Undaunted, Heydrich joined the SS and soon caught Himmler's eye. Promotion was again rapid. After being heavily involved in the planning and execution of the Night of the Long Knives and, later, the destruction of Jewish property in what became known as Kristallnacht, in 1939 he was appointed Reich protector of Bohemia and Moravia. From his base at Prague Castle he gleefully oversaw the suppression of Czech culture and the execution of Czech patriots.

His evil knew no bounds. He was the man who oversaw the work of the

Reinhard Heydrich, a portrait by Heinrich Hoffmann. (Bundesarchiv)

Einsatzgruppen, the death squads that moved in behind the victorious German armies during Operation Barbarossa. It is estimated that over two million people were murdered by these squads. Retribution was waiting for Heydrich, however, and on 27 May 1942 he was assassinated by a team of Czech agents flown in from Britain. Even from beyond the grave Heydrich's evil hand was able to wreak vengeance as the SS razed the entire villages of Lidice and Lezaky to the ground. All males over the age of sixteen were shot as a punishment for Heydrich's murder. It was a brutal conclusion to the brutal career of a brutal man.

6. BERLIN, BAVARIA AND BEYOND

Executions during the Night of the Long Knives were not restricted to Munich. Indeed, events in the Bavarian capital can be seen as simply the tip of an iceberg, acts of murder and desperation that were quickly overshadowed by what went on in other parts of Germany.

As soon as the first arrests were made at the Hotel Hanselbauer, Hitler telephoned Göring in Berlin. He gave the code word 'Hummingbird'—'*Kolibri*' in German—and by doing so launched the most intense and brutal part of the whole operation. Released from the leash, for three days Göring's police roamed Berlin and the surrounding countryside, arresting and shooting at will.

A formal hit list had been drawn up by Himmler and Göring, assisted by Theodor Eicke from Dachau and by the inscrutable but deadly Heydrich. It was a tally of people who were to be eliminated or taken out of circulation in one way or another. They were not all members of the SA and the roll call of names was added to on many occasions.

The SA, however, was a good place to start. Included on the list were the obvious people like Röhm and his deputy Edmund Heines as well as other SA men such as Karl Ernst and Oscar Heines, Edmund's younger brother. Anton von Hohberg und Buchwald was another name to feature on the list, the only member of the SS to be killed during the purge.

Von Papen was excluded as it was felt his arrest and execution would be too great a shock for ordinary Germans who still venerated the old politician. His office was ransacked, however, and his private secretary Herbert von Bosse was shot as he attempted to stop the destruction. Von Papen, when he went to Göring's office to protest, was unceremoniously flung out and placed under house arrest. His telephone was cut off and he was forbidden to make any contact with anyone in the "outside world". Perhaps sensibly, von Papen considered the situation, then said and did nothing. Perhaps for the first time he began to grasp the murderous nature of the Nazi Party—as opposed simply to its thuggishness—and the knowledge frightened him. He knew when not to rock the boat and so he bit his lip and put up with the humiliation, an act of supreme self-control that probably saved his life. It was not long before he was back in favour, being sent as Hitler's representative to the Austrian capital of Vienna where one of his first jobs was to smooth over the fuss created by the Nazi-led murder of Austrian Chancellor Engelbert Dollfuss. Counting his lucky stars, von Papen continued to serve Hitler until the end of the Third Reich.

Edgar Jung who had co-written von Papen's speech before the killings began was already in what was termed 'protective custody', having been arrested by the Gestapo two days before the putsch began. He was now murdered in his cell, purely because he had criticized the regime and the Führer. The message was simple: if you cannot get the man you really want—in this case von Papen—go for the one beneath him.

Erich Klausener, leader of Catholic Action and a man who had also been highly critical of the Führer, was shot down in his Berlin office on 30 June. As recently as 24 June he had spoken out against political oppression, albeit without naming Hitler, to an audience that numbered nearly 60,000. It was enough to decide his fate. Klausener's secretary Baroness Stotzingen and several other members of his staff were flung into the back of closed trucks and carted off to concentration camps across the country and the offices were ransacked.

Meanwhile Göring's killing squads settled eagerly to their grisly task. As soon as they were given the go-ahead they set off to arrest the people on their lists. Things did not stop at mere arrests. Men were pummelled and manhandled, beaten into

DEUTSCHE BUNDESPOST BERLIN

80 DR. ERICH KLAUSENER 1885-1934

1984

Erich Klausener, a Catholic victim of the purge, commemorated here on a postage stamp.

insensibility before they knew what was happening. The next stage soon followed with victims thrown into waiting lorries and driven out to forests and other remote locations where many of them were shot or beaten to death with pickaxes.

Göring, it soon appeared, was in the throes of a blood lust. It was the same desire to kill that had made him into one of the most renowned air aces of the Great War, only now his anger and passion were directed not at any foreign enemy but at his own countrymen. Hans Gisevius of the Prussian interior ministry and the Abwehr, witnessed Göring at work, and was later to say that the message he gave was simple: "Göring's hoarse voice booms out, 'Shoot them down. Take a whole company ... shoot them down ... just shoot them down.'"

In response to Göring's excitable, almost apoplectic tirade, over 150 SA men were arrested and taken to the police barracks in Berlin. There, within a few hours, many of them were shot, without trial, no weighing of evidence; they were on the list and so they were exterminated.

Of the dozens more that did not feature on any list it was usually too dangerous to have them suddenly arrive in prison, unannounced, unpredicted and at some stage in the future possibly even traceable. Such people were mostly killed, stabbed or beaten to death, and their bodies dumped in fields and forests, so many that the final number of men and women dispatched in this way may never be known. Only the names on the list were considered lawful killings which meant that many of those who just disappeared were victims of revenge.

With typical German efficiency the lists were worked through on a methodical basis. No argument or appeal for clemency from the victims was accepted, at least as far as their captors were concerned. There were virtually no last-minute reprieves and very few of those named managed to escape being hauled off to prison where their fate was, at best, in the balance.

Karl Ernst, one of Röhm's closest associates and a former boyfriend of the SA leader, had escaped arrest at the Hotel Hanselbauer because he had a previous engagement. On 29 June he was married and the following day was due to begin his honeymoon. The wedding and honeymoon had been arranged some time before and even Röhm could excuse him for that. Consequently, Karl Ernst was not expected at Hitler's summit meeting. Indeed, Röhm, along with Hermann Göring, actually took a break from his holiday and attended the wedding ceremony.

Röhm did not stay long in Berlin, returning to the Hotel Hanselbauer as quickly as decency allowed. He had an important appointment there the following day and not even the marriage of a close friend like Ernst was going to interfere with that!

Early on 30 June Ernst and his new wife set off to drive to Bremen where they were to board ship and take a cruise to Madeira. A car full of SS men suddenly

appeared, as if from nowhere, over-
took Ernst's car and forced it to the
side of the road. Then the SS opened
fire. His new wife and his chauffeur
were both wounded while Ernst was
smashed over the head and thrown
into the back of the SS vehicle.
Leaving the two wounded to die or
survive—they both survived—the
SS took Ernst back to the barracks
of Hitler's Personal Guard Unit in
Berlin Lichterfelde. Ernst, like so
many other SA victims, was afforded
no grace. He was shot later the same
day, believing to the end that he was
a victim of a plot by Röhm. He died
bellowing "Heil Hitler" as the bullets
slammed into his body.

Karl Ernst, shot the day after his wedding.

The official hit list had been
intended to give structure to the killings. It originally contained just sev-
enty-seven names but even Hitler had
to later admit that it had been extended because of unauthorized executions by lower
ranks in the SS. Minor civic officials became victims. One such was the town clerk from
Waldenberg, Kluno Kamphausen, killed when an SS officer who bore him a grudge
because of a failed business deal scooped him up in a trawl of victims. There were many
others as the opportunity for revenge or personal advancement suddenly appeared.

In September 1934 Himmler managed to persuade the Führer to add six names
to the list in order to maintain the sham of legality and so prevent several members of his SS from possible prosecution; although who was ever going to prosecute
them was never made public. Those extra six names brought the official tally to
eighty-three.

Other estimates place the number of victims in the hundreds. The *White Book of
Paris*, later published by German political refugees in the French capital, claimed that
401 had been executed but was only able to name just over a hundred of those killed.
In 1957 at a trial of Röhm's executioners the figure of over a thousand was bandied
about. In reality the number of the dead might be many more but an exact count has
never been made.

Among those who were murdered was Otto Ballerstedt who had previously been the leader of a secessionist party in Bavaria, one of many such small political groups. That was not his crime, however. He was the man who had been indirectly responsible for putting Hitler in prison for a month after he suffered an attack by Hitler and an SA squad during a rally in 1922. Revenge, it seemed, was not the sole preserve of the lower ranks of the Party.

Another of Hitler's targets was Gustav Ritter von Kahr whose offence against the Nazi Party had occurred so long before that he could have been excused for thinking it had been forgotten. Not as far as Hitler was concerned. Von Kahr had long since retired from politics but at the time of the Beer Hall Putsch in 1923 he had been prime minister of the region and the most powerful man in Bavaria. By reneging on his promises—albeit promises made at the point of Hitler's gun—and betraying the Nazi Party he had ensured the failure of the coup. Eventually it sealed his fate and brought him a very grisly and unpleasant death.

Exactly how or when von Kahr was killed remains unknown but he disappeared on 30 June. His body was later found in a swamp near Dachau concentration camp which seems to indicate that Eicke, the ruthless camp commandant, was involved somehow. Kahr had apparently been hacked to death with pickaxes.

A number of men were killed in order to keep them quiet. Perhaps they knew too much and were therefore regarded as a security risk, even if they had never made,

Hitler poses.

or were ever likely to make, any threat or statement that might cause problems for the Party. In the chequered past of the SA there were many incidents that probably needed covering up and this was the ideal opportunity to do just that. Karl Ernst, the SA man who had been ambushed when starting out on his honeymoon, had long been suspected of lighting the Reichstag fire and using the Dutchman van der Lubbe as a cover. Ernst had even boasted of his deed. The three SA men who had apparently assisted him in starting the fire clearly knew too much and were shot along with him.

A defrocked priest Father Bernhard Stempfle had been a fellow prisoner of Hitler's in Landsberg back in 1923 and had helped with the editing of the Führer's book *Mein Kampf*. He was another former intimate of the Nazi leader who was to suffer during the Night of the Long Knives. It had nothing to do with *Mein Kampf* but apparently Stempfle was the holder of some seriously damaging information about the death of Hitler's niece Geli Raubal.

Geli, not Eva Braun, was probably the one true love in the Führer's life and her supposed suicide in 1931 had devastated him. For some foolish reason Stempfle talked

Above left: Geli Raubal, niece of the Führer and the only woman he truly loved. Her suicide shortly before the Night of the Long Knives devastated Hitler.

Above right: Emil Maurice, chauffeur, petty criminal and one-time lover of Geli Raubal.

too much about Geli's demise, hinting that he had knowledge people would have to die for the secret to be kept. He was right, they would, but unfortunately for him it was his own death that he was predicting. His body was found in the days after the Röhm putsch in the forest of Harlaching near Munich. His neck was broken and there were three bullets in his heart. According to some sources he was killed by a murder squad led by Emil Maurice, the ex-convict who had acted as Hitler's first chauffeur and who, much to Hitler's annoyance, had also conducted an affair with Geli Raubal.

Hitler's long hand, it seemed, stretched everywhere and no one who had questioned his techniques or beliefs or opposed him in any way was safe. Gregor Strasser, despite his constant protests that he had left politics behind him, was an obvious target. He was taken into custody at noon on Saturday 30 June, the insistent rapping at the door of his Berlin house failing to warn him what was coming. He was dragged away and unceremoniously thrown into the Prinz Albrechtstrasse prison, run by the Gestapo. He did not survive too long and later that same day was executed, supposedly on the orders of Hermann Göring.

Gregor's brother Otto, never quite the same political force as his sibling, somehow managed to avoid Göring's wrath. He fled Germany and lived in exile for many years in France, Prague and Canada where he was vocal in his criticism of the Nazi regime.

Hitler salutes his troops.

Goebbels once denounced him as Nazi Germany's Public Enemy Number One and put a bounty of $500,000 on his head. He and the other Nazi leaders must have reflected that it would have been considerably easier to get rid of Otto during the Night of the Long Knives.

Other victims included people like Eugen von Kessel, a former police captain, Fritz Beck of the Munich Students' Welfare Fund and, strangely, the owner and the head waiter of the Bratwurst-Gloeckle restaurant and tavern in Munich. The inn was a favourite drinking haunt of many Nazis and was the place where Goebbels had taken part in a secret meeting with Röhm just a few days prior to the purge. The cynic might say that some Nazi official took the opportunity to wipe out his over-large bar bill but the truth is more relevant. It was felt that, like all waiters and café owners, the pair had been listening too closely to their customer's conversations. They had heard too much and despite the fact that they were not in any way political, they had to go.

And then, of course, there was former Chancellor General Kurt von Schleicher. His scheming and plotting, his attempts to split the Nazi Party and the fact that he had recently been involved in talks with Ernst Röhm—the nature of which were never disclosed—made his fate inevitable.

Von Schleicher was at home in his villa on the outskirts of Berlin when, early on Saturday 30 June, his doorbell rang. The general opened the door and was met by

Hitler, Göring and Röhm at Tempelhof airport in 1932, unusually all in civilian clothes. (Photo Bundesarchiv)

a hail of bullets fired by a squad of SS troopers dressed in civilian clothes. He died instantly. Schleicher had only recently been married, after a lifetime of bachelorhood, and now his wife Elizabeth rushed to the front door to see what was happening. She, too, was instantly shot dead.

General Kurt von Bredow, a close friend and associate of Schleicher's, met a similar end later that evening. Von Bredow had been head of the Abwehr but like his friend Schleicher had been dismissed in the days before Hitler came to power. Legend has it that on the evening of 30 June Bredow was dining at a restaurant in the centre of Berlin. Having finished his meal, he rose from the table, left a substantial tip and headed home. The waiter, a Gestapo informer, pocketed the tip, phoned the police to say their target was on the way: von Bredow was gunned down on his doorstep as soon as he reached his house.

Inevitably, the focus of interest has always been on the numbers executed or murdered during the Night of the Long Knives. Yet thousands of SA men—and others—were arrested during the purge and sent to concentration camps. Many of these were soon forgotten by the government and languished in captivity for years or until their death from supposed natural causes. Others were released whenever the mood took their captors.

There were, of course, mistakes. On the evening of Saturday 30 June Dr Willi Schmid, an eminent music critic, was seized while he was enjoying playing the cello at

Adolf Hitler with, behind him, the vacillating figure of Rudolf Hess.

his home in Munich. His wife, who was preparing dinner, and three children were also in the house but the SS took no notice of their protestations that Willi Schmid was simply a musician and critic and had nothing to do with politics. Four days later Schmid's body was returned, in a closed coffin, with orders that it should not be opened.

Dr Schmid had been mistaken for Willi Schmidt, a local SA thug who in the meantime had been arrested by another SS team and shot. In an attempt to hush up the mistake, Deputy Führer Rudolf Hess visited the grieving widow and arranged for her to receive a regular pension from the government.

Even after Hitler made news of the purge public, German newspapers tried not to disclose the names of those executed. Official radio and newspaper reports were, naturally, circumspect and for a long while the German public believed that only ten people had been killed. These included Ernst Röhm, General Schleicher and his wife, Karl Ernst and the first six SA men executed in Stadelheim prison on the orders of Adolf Hitler.

The international press, without the restrictions of state censorship, gave a more realistic figure. Over a hundred victims of the purge were listed in various newspapers at one stage or another. Even here, however, there were mistakes. One of the supposed dead was Wolf-Heinrich Graf von Helldorf, a former head of the Berlin SA. In Fact, Helldorf was not a victim but actually one of the leaders of the purge and lived on in Germany until 1944.

A newspaper cutting gives the story of the Night of the Long Knives.

Richard Wagner, seen here in Paris in 1867. His music was Hitler's inspiration.

Reporting from a distance was always going to be a process tinged or tainted by error. *Time* magazine, just one week after the purge described the death of General Schleicher in an altogether more romantic version than the reality of what was effectively just another squalid killing by a Nazi murder squad. To be fair to *Time* they did have only official German reports to go on: "According to the official Nazi version General von Schleicher resisted arrest by the Secret Police 'with a weapon in his hand.' Frau von Schleicher flung herself before her husband to protect him and the Secret Police shot them both in self-defence."

The bloodletting could not last forever and on 2 July, after three days of murder and mayhem, Hitler and Göring decided that enough was enough.

The order to cease arrests was immediately sent out and although there were one or two late killings—part of the personal vendettas that had erupted—an uneasy calm descended over Germany. The Night of the Long Knives was over but the terror in Nazi Germany had only just begun.

7. A VERY PUBLIC INTEREST AND RESPONSE

Once Goebbels and Hitler announced to the nation that a purge had taken place and that several high officials in the SA had perished—killed while resisting arrest, of course, or by committing suicide once they realized the error of their ways—there was a slight flurry of concern. It was a slight flurry only.

On the one hand everyone was pleased to see that Hitler was keeping to his promise to bring peace to the country. The SA had been too active and too violent for too long. On the other side of the coin, Hitler was unfortunately using violence to achieve that peace and some people began to question if anything was really different from the high days and holidays of Röhm's brief stretch of glory. Very few ordinary Germans voiced their concerns aloud, however, mainly because the Night of the Long Knives had seriously enhanced Hitler's power. And with the coming of that power rampant fear began to settle like falling snow across the land.

For many it was fear of the unknown rather than a face-to-face confrontation with the implements of dictatorial control but from now until the end of the Third Reich it took a very brave person indeed to question the judgement of anyone in a position of

Damage to Jewish
shops after
Kristallnacht.

authority in Germany. The atmosphere within the country settled into a strange combination of relief and concern; relief that the SA had finally been dealt with and the nagging concern which sooner or later affects all totalitarian regimes: will I be next? They were emotions not usually bandied about in public and often only acknowledged in the dead of night but, nonetheless, they were there.

Most of the German population remained ignorant of the power games, the palace intrigues and the machinations that had taken place in the build-up to the crisis. They saw everything only at the base level, as they were meant to; a troublesome nuisance had been identified and dealt with. For that they had only Adolf Hitler to thank.

In the days and weeks after the Night of the Long Knives Hitler's popularity grew immensely. He was the hero of the hour, their leader who had put his own life in danger in order to safeguard the regime and the future of Germany. He could not have designed a better or more efficient publicity campaign had he tried.

Within the Party, however, there was a degree of regret, albeit conditional, and only with some individuals. Joseph Goebbels was one significant figure who looked at the killings with a somewhat sceptical but realistic eye: "In 1934 we unfortunately failed to reform the Wehrmacht when we had the opportunity of doing so. What Röhm wanted was, of course, right in itself but in practice it could not be carried through by a homosexual and an anarchist. Had Röhm been an upright solid personality, in all probability some hundred generals rather than some hundred SA leaders would have been shot on 30 June."*

It was a realistic assessment but one that was made with the benefit of hindsight and without any great fear of contradiction. Heinrich Himmler also voiced some concerns. In a speech to Gestapo officials that October, and later published by Spartacus Educational, he declared: "For us as Secret State Police and as members of the SS, 30 June was not—as several believe—a day of victory or a day of triumph but it was the hardest day that can be visited on a soldier. To have to shoot one's own comrades, with whom one has stood side by side for eight or ten years in the struggle for an ideal, and who had then failed, is the bitterest thing which can happen to a man."

Again, Himmler was speaking from the point of view of the victor. His SS had superseded the SA and were swiftly putting themselves in an unchallengeable position where Himmler and Heydrich were soon to become mini-Hitler's in their own right. He could afford to reveal a weakness or a degree of sentiment in his attitude, however slight.

Men like Hermann Göring, ruthless and single-minded, never had any qualms about the rights or wrongs of the matter. Röhm needed to go: "There was a clique of perverted bloody revolutionaries. They are the ones who first made the Party look

---

* Spartacus Educational

The SA and Hitler Youth force Jews to clean the streets in the wake of the Kristallnacht terror.

like a pack of hoodlums with their wild orgies and beating of Jews on the streets ... It's a damned good thing that I wiped them out or they would have wiped us out."[*]

In general, the view within Germany was that a great danger had been averted. Yet there was still that niggle of doubt in the minds of many: did the so-called Röhm plot really require such a violent response? It was a question that would remain in the minds of thinking people but was not one that could be answered for many years.

Despite the fact that the Third Reich was, and always would be, a misogynistic society, from 1934 onward the women of Germany began, quite literally, to fall in love with Adolf Hitler.

It is hard to know what fatal fascination he managed to weave in the minds of his adoring female supporters—and that included most of the women in Germany—but it had undoubtedly had something to do with their view of him as their saviour. He had destroyed the SA threat, he had kept them safe in their beds at night; he was worth worshipping.

The power of the female lobby in the German home was vast and should never be underestimated. Fear of communism and of socialism, both of which they had already briefly experienced, were equalled only by fear of poverty. And Hitler was the person to shield them from those three bogeymen. The saintliness of German womanhood had nothing to do with it. Hitler was strong, he would die for them

---

* Joseph Persico, *Nuremberg: Infamy on Trial*

Left: Hitler's popularity soared after Kristallnacht, in particular with German women. This photograph shows two German women and a swastika flag.

Below: Hitler photographed with children.

and so, naturally, they would die for him. *The New York Times* was clear about the power of women in Nazi Germany: "They were the ones who incrementally brought Nazism home. They indoctrinated their children in anti-Semitism. They were the ones who would tell their children to stop playing with the Jewish children down the block."

It was a powerful legacy to emerge from the Night of the Long Knives and cemented Hitler's position almost to the end of his days as chancellor and Führer. It may not have been something he planned for or intended but when it occurred he was ruthless enough to seize the situation with both hands and exploit it to the full.

*

The international response was varied. Hitler's regime was unpopular, feared even, in many parts of Europe. That dislike was now augmented by a large measure of disgust. The disgust was directed, in particular, at the gangster methods that had been employed during the purge and, perhaps more than anything, at the arbitrary judgement used to rid the country of Ernst Röhm.

If ever there was a case of double standards this was it, in spades. Many governments and their representatives—diplomats and statesmen—who had come into contact with them, had little time for the thuggish, brutal Röhm or his brawling SA battalions but this was a pretty big stick that had fallen unexpectedly into their laps. And it was

A cartoon from a British newspaper. The caption says, "It seems they salute with two arms these days."

just the size and shape with which to beat the Nazi Party. When everything was considered it was not a tool that anyone could afford to pass by.

Double standards did not just apply to foreign governments. In one of his first orders of the day to Lutze, the new SA leader, Hitler was clear that he expected Lutze to rebuild an organization where every German mother could be sure that, if they joined the SA, her children would not be corrupted in any way.

Given the past history of Röhm and the ongoing and enormous over-indulgences of Party leaders like Göring and Julius Streicher, it seemed a dangerous comment to make but Hitler was now working from a position of great strength and he could afford to take more risks.

The new SA was to be a model of modesty and decorum. Despite having been aware for years about the rampant homosexuality at the top of the SA—Röhm's deputy Heines was known throughout the organization by the nickname of Fraulein Schmidt—Hitler now seized the moral high ground. Having attained it, it was a position he was never inclined to relinquish.

Whatever Hitler did to his opponents, it was the lack of remorse that had most horrified the democratic countries of Europe. The Nazi government was not merely unapologetic, it was also intensely proud of its actions.

Joseph Stalin was later, after the Second World War had ended and retribution was still swirling in the air, to advocate giving war criminals at Nuremberg a swift but fair

Hitler, Göring and supporting industrialists who are happy to continue pouring money into the Party coffers now that Röhm has gone.

trial before they were then taken out and shot. The democratic nations would probably have been happy to see such a process taking place in Germany in 1934 but after the Night of the Long Knives there were no trials and no investigations, just executions.

Initial reports in European and U.S. newspapers were, as might be expected, little more than verbatim accounts of who had been shot, who had been arrested and so on. But as more and more information began to seep out of Germany so the criticism, praise and appraisals began.

The Bethlehem Globe-Times of Pennsylvania was almost complementary when, on 2 July 1934, its headline writers came up with this: "Believed 500 are killed in German Revolt: Hitler, in relentless executions, kills off leaders in an attempt to suppress the Second Revolution." The paper almost got it right but not quite. *The New York Times* initially called the purge "swift and decisive" but a few days later, as more information was gathered and as reality set in, the language and the opinion of the writers at the paper changed. Now, instead of praising Hitler they used phrases like "firing squad justice".

With authors like Dr Edward J. Ping, writing in *The Wall Street Journal*, issuing warnings that Hitler might have to become even more ruthless in order to maintain power, people in the U.S. began to see that things in Europe were not as simple as they first appeared. Indeed, there was a growing belief that the German take on fascism—unlike Mussolini's regime in Italy—was potentially very dangerous indeed.

In Britain the right-wing *Daily Mail* was equally as blasé as were the early comments from the U.S. Hitler, the paper said, had saved his country: "Swiftly and with exorable severity, he has delivered Germany from men who had become a danger to the unity of the German people and to the order of the state. With lightning rapidity he has caused them to be removed from high office, to be arrested, and put to death. The names of the men who have been shot by his orders are already known. Hitler's love of Germany has triumphed over private friendships and fidelity to comrades who had stood shoulder to shoulder with him in the fight for Germany's future."

Considering the political stance of Lord Rothermere, owner of *The Mail*, and events like the recent General Strike in Britain, it is not too difficult to read the sub-text to the article. In the years ahead Rothermere went on to support Oswald Mosley's Blackshirts—"Hurrah for the Blackshirts," his paper once trumpeted. The excesses of Mosley and the British Union of Fascists eventually put even Lord Rothermere off supporting the British version of fascism. However, it was not before Goebbels was able to use many of the paper's leading articles as propaganda pieces.

Part of the problem was that many editors at the time were unable to differentiate between politics and personal life. The socialist *Manchester Guardian*, a paper which twelve months earlier had led with a comment about the SA—"Their chief weapon is terror"—was scathing about Röhm's sexual activities, linking the SA chief's sexual corruption with his supposed plot to depose Hitler.

Hurrah for the Blackshirts

By VISCOUNT ROTHERMERE

BECAUSE Fascism comes from Italy, shortsighted people in this country think they show a sturdy national spirit by deriding it.

If their ancestors had been equally stupid, Britain would have had no banking system, no Roman law, nor even any football, since all of these are of Italian invention.

✦ ✦ ✦

THE Socialists, especially who jeer at the principles and uniform of the Blackshirts as being of foreign origin, forget that the founder and High Priest of their own creed was the German Jew Karl Marx.

Though the name and form of Fascism originated in Italy, that movement is not now peculiar to any nation.

and disgusted by the incompetence of their elders in dealing with the depression that has followed on it. The other is made up of men too young to remember the war but ready to put all their ardour and energy at the service of a cause which offers them a vigorous constructive policy in place of the drift and indecision of the old political parties.

Blackshirts proclaim a fact which politicians dating from pre-war days will never face—that the new age requires new methods and new men. They base their contention on the

views" were an effective substitute in human affairs for action, the National Government would be the best that Britain has ever had. But the experience of the past two-years has proved that these futile and time-wasting devices are no more than a screen for inertia and indecision.

✦ ✦ ✦

THE huge majority obtained by the present Government at the general election of 1931 was the last vote of confidence that the nation will, ever, give to Old Gang politicians. Two years from now another general election will be almost due. The whole future of Britain will depend upon its issue.

A prolongation of the present régime may be regarded, in the country's present mood, as out of the question. There will be a pronounced swing either to Right or Left.

Crazy News Reel

Presented by D. B. WYNDHAM LEWIS

OLD soldiers will note, with satisfaction, one of the Morland group, at the British Art Exhibition, "The Soldier's Return."

The handsome, even foppish, soldier, wearing an expensive shirt and a natty velvet neckband, and looking like Squire Thornhill, is evidently his humble and astonished relatives became quartermaster-sergeant, and is now going to buy the village. His father waggishly holds out to him a mug of rum. He ignores it. Rum is

The *Daily Mail*'s right-wing take on events.

One American journalist even went so far as to write that every single senior SA officer was a practising homosexual. He had no proof but the remark undoubtedly sold papers. And it was unlikely to have had any effect on the culling and killing in Germany.

When all was said and done, however, the results of the purge have to be considered in line with the predominantly pacifist attitudes of most governments at the time.

The Great War had brought conflict like nobody had ever seen or imagined before, over sixteen million casualties being incurred in a war that lasted just four years. That blood-letting was less than twenty years in the past and no one wanted a repetition of anything like that.

This was the age of the appeasers when all right-thinking politicians would do almost anything to avoid another conflict. Unfortunately, Hitler was no 'right-thinking politician' and nobody was willing to admit that he was not the sort of man you could do business with.

Hitler's long-term political and military plans had already been laid, the overriding aim being to create living space for the German people in the east. It was an aim that nobody recognized until the might of the Wehrmacht was unleashed on the Soviets in 1941, not even the Soviets who still believed that they could negotiate with the man and his government.

Despite the barbaric nature of the reprisals, the killings without trial and the total lack of remorse, nobody could quite believe that Hitler and the Nazis would behave like that abroad.

Foreign policy was a very different beast from affairs at home, the politicians of the 1930s felt. It needed delicate diplomacy and tact and was not something that a bankrupt and beaten country like Germany was ever going to risk getting wrong.

The treason, if there was any, and the subsequent execution of Röhm and his SA leaders was an internal affair, a problem for Hitler and the German government.

Leave them to it. Diplomats and democratic governments believed—and kept on believing until it was too late—that they could still do business with the Führer.

Only after the war did the reality of the situation really make itself felt. Even regional newspapers like The *Dundee Courier* were soon stating: "Within 18 months of coming to power, the meek looking Hitler showed his tiger claws in the notorious 'night of the long knives' when Röhm and his associates were liquidated." No platitudes there, no attempts to gloss over the barbarity. Röhm and his comrades are liquidated. Hitler is not acting for the good of his country; he is displaying his "tiger claws". And the killings are not just unacceptable, they are notorious.

Nobody quite understood that Hitler was in fact a gambler, perhaps the greatest gambler the world had ever seen. He would continue to gamble—with his country and its people, with his reputation and, ultimately, with his own life. Of course he would take risks in his foreign policy; it was as natural to him as walking. And that was something the democratic countries of the world failed to see until it was almost too late.

In the wake of the Second World War, people were clear what they believed—a few dead Nazis? Well, they got what they deserved. Hitler would have probably turned in his grave and smiled to himself. It was all part of the decadence that he seen for years and hated.

The Nazis and the Cinema

Most people have heard of Leni Riefenstahl's *Triumph of the Will* and the other Nazi propaganda films of the 1930s. These short but powerful visual clips were hurled again and again at the viewing public, their repeated slogans being aimed at the emotions of the audience. It was, really, an exercise in power. The Party message was the main purpose behind them: anti-Semitism and *lebensraum*. Small wonder that Goebbels used film to explain such events as the Night of the Long Knives.

However, what got the German people into the cinemas in the first place was not the propaganda films from the ministry of Joseph Goebbels. It was the thought of the big picture, the main drama that they were about to watch. And Goebbels was clear that such offerings were to be "entertaining and glamorous". Goebbels was patron of the German film industry and from the early stages of the Party knew that it was important to keep the public in good spirits. It was, he believed, failure of morale that had led directly to German defeat in the Great War. Rather than have such a thing happen in Nazi Germany, Goebbels knew he had to act: he would provide escapism at a time when Germany seemed to be wallowing in its own self-destructive mud.

The offerings given to the German public were rarely foreign productions, most of them being locally produced. As a result the films were heavily censored and as the 1930s progressed, were being made by a decreasing number of directors and actors; inevitable as many of the most talented filmmakers had either left the country or were incarcerated in concentration camps.

With the entire film industry becoming subordinated to Goebbels's ministry of propaganda, the films that were produced were lightweight but all contained the subliminal messages that confirmed the Nazi ideals. Include unabashed anti-Semitic films like *Jew Süss* (based on the story of Joseph Süss Oppenheimer, an 18th-century court Jew in the employ of Duke Karl Alexander of Württemberg) that screened in the 5,000 cinemas across the country, and it was simple to convert the unsubtle indoctrination into raw hatred.

Membership of the Reichsfilmkanner was mandatory for all filmmakers but by the late 1930s the German film industry was in trouble. With exports having dropped, mainly due to foreign boycotts and poor-quality productions, it was becoming more and more expensive to make movies. The result was fewer films for the public to watch. It did not trouble Goebbels unduly. The purpose of the main feature was to hook the audience in order to promote the propaganda of the short pieces; any benefit to be gained from the feature was a bonus. Hitler knew the power of film. His own late-night viewing at the Berghof has been well documented. And even when Germany was being systematically dismembered by Allied bombers, an evening at the cinema was still being promoted as good escapism, with Goebbels insisting that all cinemas should be opened immediately following an air raid.

Leni Riefenstahl confers on set with Heinrich Himmler. (Bundesarchiv)

8. AFTERMATH

As far as the Nazi Party was concerned, the Night of the Long Knives had, at the most basic level, headed off a potential army coup; at best it had brought the Reichswehr closer than ever to the centre of Nazi politics and to control by Party leaders. The irony of the situation with the murder of Ernst Röhm managing to achieve much of what the SA leader had always wanted was a factor that was not lost on Hitler and the members of his inner circle. The fact that an organization like the army which had always prided itself on honour and decency had allowed the government of the country to exact gangster revenge and street-corner justice on beaten opponents was barely noted. Where it was, such niceties were immediately forgotten anyway. The military had, without doubt, signed a pact with the Devil.

So deep was the army's desire to preserve its independence and power that its commanders allowed the cold-blooded murder of two of its own generals, von Schleicher and von Bredow, to go unpunished and barely even acknowledged. The two martyred generals were, as far as the army high command was concerned, merely collateral damage and an edict or order was issued stating that no Wehrmacht officer was to

A propaganda photograph showing a member of the Hitler Youth with his swastika flag.

go to their funerals. The order was obeyed apart from one general who had already resigned his post and whose actions were, therefore, immaterial.

Similarly, the law practices of the country and the two churches of Germany, Catholic and Lutheran, did not raise protest of any kind. This was despite the fact that the leader of Catholic Action, Erich Klausener, had been one of the many victims. In the years ahead the Catholic Church was to bitterly regret its indecision at such a time.

And what about the law and the judiciary, people were to later ask? It was another meek surrender, the foremost legal brain in the country even going so far as to publish an article praising Hitler for his actions in defending the law. It was the start of a long and decidedly shady road for the German legal profession, a road that reached its nadir in the ludicrous show trials following the bomb plot against Hitler in 1944. Embracing the Nazi regime, the actions of the legal profession as a whole had little to commend it and the future behaviour of many of Hitler's judges would have been farcical had it not been so tragic.

Governance of the country was something else that was about to change. A few months after the Night of the Long Knives President Hindenburg died on 2 August 1934. Almost immediately a law was enacted combining the positions of president and chancellor. The powers and prestige of president were thus neatly transferred to the Führer and the final nail in Hitler's dictatorship was hammered in. His joy when all members of the armed forces swore an oath of loyalty to him, rather than to his position, must have made all the years of sacrifice more than satisfying: "I swear by God this sacred oath, that I will render unconditional obedience to Adolf Hitler, the Führer of the German Reich and people ... and will be ready as a brave soldier to risk my life at any time for this oath."

The army which, realistically, was now the only group capable of destroying the Nazis had effectively tied itself to the Führer's apron strings. It was something of a Devil's Deal and was a knot that would last almost to the end.

Even President Hindenburg, army to the bones, had been appreciative of Hitler's actions. Before his death and while the executions and arrests were still taking place, he had sent a telegram to the Führer, expressing his thanks: "I gather from reports submitted to me that by energetic intervention you courageously, at the risk of your own life, suppressed all treasonable machinations at the outset; you saved the German people from grave danger."

Whether or not the dying president actually penned that telegram, or whether he even knew of its existence, is immaterial. It showed that from now on the higher echelons of German society and government were behind the Nazis and behind Adolf Hitler in particular, all the way to the gates of Hell.

By effectively destroying the power of the SA, Hitler had not markedly made Germany a safer place but he had made his own regime considerably more powerful and more secure. Gone was any possibility of a second revolution, gone was the charismatic and threatening figure of Ernst Röhm, gone was any last vestige of democracy. And yet the SA, or at least the vast bulk of it, survived the Night of the Long Knives. The purge did not destroy Röhm's private army; it merely took out its leaders, reduced it in size and eliminated anyone who might be inclined to assist Röhm in his machinations, actual or intended, mythical or fictional.

The SA could not continue in its original form, however. Destruction of the organization was central to Hitler's web of deceit and in the months after the purge the SA was totally revamped and changed. Hitler was no longer prepared to endure the pressures inflicted by three or four million members of a paramilitary organization and, consequently, the SA was greatly reduced in numbers. The organization survived until well into the war years, however, the last few members being amal-

gamated into a special tank unit to fight the advancing Russians in 1944. By then everyone and anyone able to hold a rifle had been drafted into the army. The last few members of the SA were no different from anyone else.

Victor Lutze, the SA officer who had accompanied Hitler to the Hotel Hanselbauer on the morning of 30 June, became the SA's new chief of staff just a few days after Röhm's death. It was a prize for his loyalty to Hitler.

Lutze was the perfect choice: unassuming, more interested in his family than in politics and never likely to offer any sort of threat to Adolf Hitler. He agreed completely with the Führer's first directive regarding the reorganization of the SA, a memo which stated that "SA men should be leaders, not ludicrous apes."

Significantly for the future of Nazi Germany, the SS was formally split from the SA and became a totally

Victor Lutze, the man who took over control of the SA after Röhm's murder.

separate entity with Himmler as its Reichsführer. It was a mere technicality as they had been operating as a separate entity for a long time now but from 20 July 1934 the SS was responsible only to Hitler and, of course, its own arch-druid, Heinrich Himmler.

Being by nature indolent and inclined towards procrastination rather than action, the creation of what was, almost literally, his own Praetorian Guard gave Hitler a huge sense of security.

And yet he had little control over or involvement with the SS, leaving its day-to-day running to other people. All Hitler was concerned about was the overall effect or image of his black-uniformed guards and the use to which they could, if needed, be put. It was a definite nod in the direction of Heydrich and Himmler.

Following the Röhm purge, the SA lost its aircraft, its skirmisher and its motor branches and became something of a training or prep school for the armed forces. It still had a role in propping up the regime, appearing in jackboots and uniforms at rallies or marches, and, as Hitler's noose tightened around German throats, it was still instrumental in the process of intimidating, humiliating and punishing Jews and political opponents.

One of the most significant events in SA history took place on 9 November 1938, long after the original purge that had supposedly weakened their standing. This was *Kristallnacht*, the night of broken glass, an outburst of government-sponsored anti-Semitic rioting and violence that followed the assassination of the German diplomat Ernst von Rath in Paris. The assassin was a young Jew by the name of Herschel Feibel Grynszpan, exacting revenge on the Nazi regime for the forced deportation of his family from Hamburg. The violence that immediately erupted was widespread with Hitler happily unleashing the SA in what was to be one of its last orgies of unrestricted terror.

More than 300 synagogues were looted, vandalized and burned across greater Germany—Germany, Austria and the Sudetenland—nearly a hundred innocent Jewish citizens were killed and somewhere in the region of 20,000 Jewish men were arrested. Many of these were sent to concentration camps where many of them duly died. Over 800 Jewish shops were looted and destroyed. Again, under instruction, the police and the army stood by and watched as the wave of destruction spread across the country.

In a strange, not to say unbelievable, twist of fate the SA was declared a 'non-criminal' organization at the Nuremberg War Crimes trials held after the war. After the Night of the Long Knives, the SA was not, the tribunal ruled, the force it had once been, and never would be despite growing in size once more as the Second World War approached. Most significantly of all, the SA outrages during Kristallnacht marked the beginning of the systematic persecution of the Jews, something that had been merely played at before.

Sadistically, the German Jews were fined and made to pay for the damage inflicted by the SA on city buildings, a figure that eventually reached one billion marks. Such ridiculously unlawful and punitive measures might, with hindsight, seem almost beyond belief. But that is exactly what happened at the end of 1938.

The oppression went further. Jews could no longer own or even drive a car. They were forbidden to attend theatres or movies or use public parks and swimming pools. Even their wireless sets were confiscated. And people in all walks of German life still said that the power of the SA had been broken. It was a hopeless delusion.

More than anything, the Night of the Long Knives was a clear indication of what would happen to anyone who dared raise a hand against the Party. If they did not know it before, it was now clearly apparent to any prospective opponents that Hitler would stop at nothing to retain his position at the head of the German state.

What is almost unbelievable is the sad fact that foreign powers, in particular the United States, Great Britain and France, failed to see that what Hitler had done at home, he could also do abroad. Nobody learned lessons from the Night of the Long Knives and that is the ultimate tragedy of the purge.

High-ranking Nazis and SS members during one of Himmler's visits to Mauthausen concentration camp. Himmler was the ultimate beneficiary of the SA purge. (Bundesarchiv)

9. WHERE DID THEY GO?

So many men and women were involved, one way or another, in the Night of the Long Knives that it is sometimes difficult to assimilate quite who they were and what happened to them, particularly the 'minor' characters in the drama. The following list does not claim to be definitive but it does give some account of the players, named in the text, and who took part in what was a seminal moment in Nazi and German history. Major figures like Hitler, Röhm, and Göring etc. are not listed as their histories and future careers are well enough known:

- Max Amann was Hitler's sergeant during the Great War, he became the first business manager of the Nazi Party, a member of the Reichstag and Reich press leader. After the war he was sentenced to ten years in a labour camp, released in 1953 and died, in poverty, in Munich in 1957.
- Otto Ballerstedt was leader of an obscure nationalist sect, the Bayernbund; he was physically assaulted by Hitler in 1922 which caused the Nazi leader to serve a month in gaol. He was shot in the back of the head during the Night of the Long Knives, probably at Dachau concentration camp.
- Hans Baur, Hitler's personal pilot, was a decorated air ace from the Great War. He had no interest in politics but Hitler, who disliked flying, trusted his ability as a pilot. Baur later wrote a book, *I Was Hitler's Pilot*, about his experiences.
- Fritz Beck was a political activist, founder of the International Students' Relief Centre and a known opponent of the Nazi Party. His body, with five bullet holes in it, was found dumped in fields with bruises and other marks of ill treatment on his torso.
- General Werner von Blomberg was minister of defence under Hitler until a scandal forced his resignation. His new, second wife, it was discovered, had been a prostitute. Blomberg went into retirement, missed the war and died in 1946.
- Herbert von Bose was head of the press division under von Papen, and a known opponent of the Nazi Party. Shot ten times as he was being interrogated or, as the SS claimed, when he tried to prevent them wrecking von Papen's office.
- Anton Drexler, the founder member of the German Workers' Party, was something of a mentor to the inexperienced Hitler. Poet and political activist, he was increasingly sidelined as Hitler grew in power. Not considered significant enough to suffer in the purge, Drexler died in 1942.

- Otto Dietrich was press chief of the Nazi Party, and was with Hitler when Röhm was arrested. Never known for the accuracy of his reporting, he suffered a nervous breakdown during the war and afterward was sentenced to seven years in prison.
- Theodor Eicke, commandant of Dachau concentration camp during the purge, was undoubtedly involved in many of the executions. He was killed in February 1943 when his Fieseler Storch aircraft was shot down over Russia.
- Matthias Erzberger, despite being politically and emotionally opposed to the Treaty of Versailles, signed the document as an authorized signatory for the Weimar Republic. In retaliation, he was assassinated by a right-wing group of terrorists in August 1921.

Herbert von Bosse, yet another victim of the Night of the Long Knives.

- Hans Gisevius, diplomat and a covert opponent of the Nazi Party, was, first, a member of the Prussian interior ministry and then the Abwehr. He was involved in the 20 July plot against Hitler. When it failed he fled to Switzerland, thus becoming one of the few plotters to survive.
- Ulrich Graf, an amateur wrestler and petty criminal who acted as Hitler's bodyguard, was one of the earliest members of the Nazi Party. After the war, Graf was sentenced to five years' hard labour by a West German court. He died in 1950.
- Herschel Grynszpan was the seventeen-year-old Jewish student who assassinated Ernst von Rath in Paris in 1938. Sent to Sachsenhausen concentration camp, his fate is unknown but he probably died in the camp during the war years.
- Wolff-Heinrich Graf von Helldorf, the police official and politician mistakenly thought to have been killed during the Night of the Long Knives, became disenchanted with the Nazi regime and was hanged for his part in the 20 July plot against Hitler in 1944.
- Heinrich Hoffmann became the official photographer for Adolf Hitler and made millions from selling images of the Führer. After the war he was sentenced to four years in prison for war profiteering.

Salzburg, 1938: Fertile Nazi recruiting ground, the office for the unemployed. (Annemarie Schwarzenbach/ Swiss Literary Archives)

- Eric Kempka was Hitler's principal chauffeur from 1934 until 1945. Kempka was present in the Führer bunker when Hitler shot himself in April 1945 and obtained the gasoline to burn the bodies of the Führer and Eva Braun.
- Eugen von Kessel, a former policeman, was running a German news bureau in 1934. The motives for his death are not clear but it has been said that Heydrich himself went to Kessel's office and carried out the shooting.
- Michael Lippert, deputy to Theodor Eicke at Dachau, took part in the shooting of Röhm. Later commandant of several different concentration camps, in 1957 he was sentenced to eighteen months' imprisonment for his part in the murder of Ernst Röhm.
- Marinus van der Lubbe, the Dutch communist accused of setting fire to the Reichstag in 1933, was guillotined to death but there has always been doubt about his involvement in the fire.
- Victor Lutze, successor to Ernst Röhm as chief of staff of the SA, was killed in a car crash in May 1943, a victim of his own reckless driving, in contrast to his submissive personality

- Emil Maurice, founder member of the SS, one of the few Nazis to have part-Jewish, part-Aryan German heritage, served in the Luftwaffe during the war and later sentenced to four years' hard labour by a West German court. He died in 1972.
- Oswald Mosley, British peer and MP, first for the Conservative Party then as an Independent, then as a member of Labour, founded the right-wing New Party which merged with the British Union of Fascists. The BUF was banned during the war and Mosley was imprisoned.
- Ernst von Rath was the German diplomat who was assassinated, shot five times by Herschel Grynszpan in Paris in 1938. On Hitler's orders, von Rath—who was just a junior diplomat—was promoted to Legal Counsel First Class on his deathbed. Accusations of homosexuality arose after his death.
- Lord Rothermere, or Harold Sydney Harmsworth, was a British newspaper tycocn who was a supporter of right-wing politics. He supported the Nazi Party, giving them publicity in his *Daily Mail*, believing that they would help restore the German monarchy. He died in November 1940.
- Wilhelm 'Willi' Schmid, renowned German music critic, founder of the Munich Viol Quartet, was perhaps the most unfortunate victim of the purge. After his death, arrested and shot by mistake, his wife immigrated to the U.S. where she became a citizen in 1944.
- Karl Wolff, senior SS commander and Heinrich Himmler confidant, finished the war as supreme commander of all SS forces in Italy. Convicted of war crimes in 1964, he was released five years later.

There were many others involved, in one way or another, in the Night of the Long Knives. For some it was just a peripheral involvement, for others—like Göring and Himmler—it was an essential element in their charge up the ranks of the Nazi Party. Whether or not there was ever a plot against the regime remains unclear. But there could have been, that was the point for Hitler and his cronies. Röhm had the manpower and the temperament to launch a coup at some stage—maybe not in 1934 but in the future. When the time was ripe he could have struck and made a grab for power. It remains speculation but for Hitler, to leave him alive and the SA intact, was a risk not worth taking.

CONCLUSION

It has often been claimed that most revolutions invariably require a second upsurge, a second revolution as it is sometimes called. If that is so then the Night of the Long Knives probably fitted the bill as far as Nazi Germany was concerned. The Röhm purge effectively eliminated many of the elements that had been crucial to the success of the first revolution, notably the rough and uncouth SA or Brownshirts which had, in a spectacular and dramatic fashion, helped barrel Hitler into the position of supreme power.

Inevitably Hitler and the Nazi leaders changed their attitudes and behaviour as they tasted the pleasures of success. Never losing sight of their basic principles, outwardly at least they had to alter their stance to accommodate the people and the places they encountered. Sadly, the SA was not able to change with them.

The second revolution, if that is what it was, killed off more than just the power of the SA. It also destroyed Ernst Röhm who was always too brutal and outspoken for government duty but who was more than capable of leading a putsch against Adolf Hitler. Within the SA his popularity certainly rivalled the Führer's. Hitler might have been slow to see it but, eventually, it became apparent that, between them, Röhm and the SA represented a clear and present danger.

Part of Röhm's problem was that he simply could not keep his mouth closed. He bragged, he threatened, he promised his version of a second revolution—and part of that second, socialist revolution involved subsuming the German army into the ranks of his own paramilitary force. That fact, more than anything, ensured that sooner or later Hitler would be forced to act against him.

Germany had always been a martial society. Modern Germany had been founded or created by Otto von Bismarck on traditions, rules and routines that were rooted in Prussian militarism. Until the 1914–18 war the German army had been the strongest military force in the world. It is small wonder that for the first few months of that war the German army, racing through Belgium in the offensive known as the Schlieffen plan, had trampled everything before it. The army gave the country strength and occupied a position of importance within German society that was hard for other nations to understand. Any attempt to attack its standing was bound to create major difficulties, something that Ernst Röhm simply did not grasp, despite the fact that he had served as an officer in that same army for many years.

The need to placate the wealthy industrialists and capitalists who had bankrolled the Party—and were continuing to do so—simply added to the 'Röhm problem'.

By 1934 Hitler could afford to do without Röhm; he could not afford to do without his financial backers. The second revolution did indeed come but it was not Röhm's imagined violent uprising. It was a far more gradual process that began with Röhm's death and ended with the establishment of Hitler's totalitarian dictatorship.

The Night of the Long Knives demonstrated Hitler's ruthlessness. Old friends, Party comrades of many years standing, politicians, statesmen and generals, they were all potential victims the moment their usefulness was over.

The tragedy for the world was that nobody seemed to understand Hitler's ability to transfer that ruthlessness from Germany to the world stage. Very few politicians and statesmen recognized that this was no local tinpot dictator, content with establishing a power base in Germany. This was a man with ideas of world domination, a man who would continue to play the role of the great gambler right to the end.

What marked down the Night of the Long Knives as different was the ruthless and deadly approach by all of the Nazi leaders. From now on nobody was retired from

The Hitler Youth marches.

A rare protest at Hitler's territorial demands in Europe.

duty, or very few of them at least. Political opponents were simply shot or incarcerated in concentration camps.

Such carnage had not been seen in Europe for hundreds of years, and for it to happen in the country that had spawned Beethoven, Goethe, and Wagner made it doubly terrifying. Or perhaps it did not. Adolf Hitler's favourite reading material was a series of cowboy books about a vengeful and sadistic character called Old Shatterhand, a man who roamed the Wild West looking for potential victims: a far cry from the poems of Goethe.

The music of Wagner was important to Hitler but he never really understood it. To him it was all about glory, spectacle and the re-emergence of the Germanic people. It was martial and it was self-sacrificing. The quality of the music was immaterial.

To the watching world it seemed as if the Nazi Party had ditched culture along with the books that had been burned in the plazas. And with that culture went tolerance and justice; with it went civilization.

There was worse to come, far worse, but the Night of the Long Knives retains a resonance to frighten and appal. The world did not learn its lesson in 1934 but if the only real purpose behind studying history is to learn from mistakes then there is still time.

BIBLIOGRAPHY

I make no apologies for including Alan Bullock's *Hitler: A Study in Tyranny* and William L. Shirer's *The Rise and Fall of the Third Reich* in the list of books/ authors I read and have occasionally quoted from in this study. They are still two of the best and most vivid accounts of Hitler's Germany that it is possible to find, works to study and to enjoy even though it is some years since they were first published.

Books
Anon, *Bartlett's Fantastic Quotations*, MacMillan, London, 1955
Baur, Hans, *I Was Hitler's Pilot*, Pen & Sword, Barnsley, 2013
Bullock, Alan, *Hitler: A Study in Tyranny*, Pelican, London, 1962
Cantrell, Rebecca, *A Night of Long Knives,* Harper Collins, New York, 2017
Carradice, Phil, *An Illustrated Introduction to the First World War*, Amberley, Stroud, 2014
Hughes, Richard, *The Fox in the Attic*, Chatto & Windus, London, 1961
Kershaw, Ian, *Hitler: Hubris 1889 to 1936*, Allen Lane, London, 1998
Knopp, Guido, *Hitler's Women*, Sutton Publishing, Stroud, 2006
Persico, Joseph, *Nuremberg: Infamy on Trial*, Allison & Busby, London, 1995
Rees, Laurence, *The Dark Charisma of Adolf Hitler*, Ebury Press, London, 2013
River, Charles (Ed.), *The Night of the Long Knives*, Charles River Editions, Boston, 2017
Ryback, Timothy W., *Hitler's Private Library*, Bodley Head, London, 2009
Schnaubelt, Eric, 'The Night of the Long Knives,' paper for University of Santa Barbara, 2009
Shirer, William L. & Ron Rosenbaum, *The Rise and Fall of the Third Reich*, (electronic edition), New York, 2011
Shirer, William L., *The Rise and Fall of the Third Reich*, Pan Books, London, 1960
Wighton, Charles & Gunter Peis, *They Spied on England*, Odhams, London, 1958
Wilson, A. N., *Hitler, A Short Biography*, Harper Collins, London 2012

Documentaries
Hitler: A Profile, SBS, 1995
The World at War, Granada Television, 1973–74

Periodicals
Daily Mail (1934)
Dundee Courier (1952)

History Revealed (BBC) (various)
Manchester Guardian (1933 & 1934)
The Bethlehem Globe-Times (1934)
The Guardian (2003)
The New York Times (1934 and 1997)
The Wall Street Journal (1934)
Time magazine (various)
World Histories (BBC, various)

Websites

http://spartcus-educational.com/GERnight.htm
https://daily.jstar.org/ernst-Röhm-the-highest-ranking-gay-Nazi
https://en.wikipedia.org/wiki/Night-of-the-Long-Knives
https://en.wikipedia.org/wiki/Victims-of-the-Night-of-the-Long-Knives
hwww.jewishvirtuallibrary.org/women-of-the-third-reich
www.ushman.org/wic/en/article.php

SS death camp staff, this group at Belzec, Poland.

Index

Acknowledgements

Sincere thanks to the following: the staff of Cardiff Central Library, Penarth Library and Pembrokeshire County Library; my sons Andrew and Douglas for their helpful and, more often than not, sceptical comments and opinions—thanks for keeping my feet on the ground, boys; my old friend Roger MacCallum for his knowledge and, above all, his ability in technology, a skill that still leaves me gasping in amazement— one day, mate, I'll be able to translate your teaching into action; my brother-in-law Lewis Hughes: thanks for all those conversations over a glass or two, conversations that may have begun with Hitler and the SA but invariably ended by covering a wide range of British and world history. Thanks to Trudy, my darling, your memory as inspirational as always. We just didn't have enough time but at least you taught me to love Bavaria, the Black Forest and the Rhine. I hope it comes through in this book.

Phil Carradice is a poet, novelist and historian. He has written over fifty books, the most recent being *The Call-up: A Study of Peacetime Conscription in Britain* and *Napoleon in Defeat and Captivity*. He presents the BBC Wales history programme *The Past Master* and is a regular broadcaster on both TV and radio. A native of Pembroke Dock, he now lives in the Vale of Glamorgan but travels extensively in the course of his work. Educated at Cardiff University and at Cardiff College of Education, Phil is a former head teacher but now lives as a full-time writer and is regarded as one of Wales's best creative writing tutors. He writes extensively for several Pen & Sword military history series including 'Cold War 1945–1991' and 'History of Terror'.